SWEETER BY THE DOZEN

SWEETER
BY THE DOZEN
Making Jesus the Lord of Our Family Size

RANDALL HEKMAN

Reformation Heritage Books
Grand Rapids, Michigan

Reformation Heritage Books
2965 Leonard St. NE
Grand Rapids, MI 49525
616-977-0889
orders@heritagebooks.org
www.heritagebooks.org

Unless otherwise indicated, Scripture taken from the New King James Version®. Copyright © 1982 by Thomas Nelson. Used by permission. All rights reserved.

Printed in the United States of America
19 20 21 22 23 24/10 9 8 7 6 5 4 3 2 1

Library of Congress Cataloging-in-Publication Data

Names: Hekman, Randall J., author.
Title: Sweeter by the dozen : making Jesus the lord of our family size / Randall Hekman.
Description: Grand Rapids, Michigan : Reformation Heritage Books, 2019. | Includes bibliographical references.
Identifiers: LCCN 2019041123 | ISBN 9781601787538 (paperback) | ISBN 9781601787545 (epub)
Subjects: LCSH: Family planning—Religious aspects—Christianity. | Family size—Religious aspects—Christianity.
Classification: LCC HQ766.25 .H45 2019 | DDC 241/.663—dc23
LC record available at https://lccn.loc.gov/2019041123

For additional Reformed literature, request a free book list from Reformation Heritage Books at the above regular or email address.

CONTENTS

PART FOUR
Conclusion

FOREWORD

My friend of many years, whom I respectfully call Judge Hekman due to his God-honoring work as a judge in our community, is a no nonsense kind of guy. I treasure my friendship in Christ with him. He is a joy to be with, but I warn you in love: his views are biblical and strong when it comes to subjects like the need for prayer and revival, the atrociousness of baby-killing in the womb (which we rather politely call abortion), and our calling to surrender all of life to the lordship of Christ—including the area of our family size, which is the subject of this rather provocative, challenging, yet winsome book.

Judge Hekman writes on this volatile subject from deep personal experience as a father of twelve children. He felt led by God to give up some of his greatest personal ambitions in order to submit to Christ's lordship with regard to having more children, if the Lord would so direct. His story is winsomely told in these pages (Part One), after which he unpacks what Scripture has to say about childbearing and childrearing (Part Two). In the final part of his book, he responds to ten kickback arguments that husbands and wives (including a goodly number of Christians) have against letting Christ be the Lord of the number of children He wishes to loan and bequeath to them to be raised for Him.

There is a good way and a bad way to read this book. The bad way is to pick apart every statement that the good Judge makes that you don't immediately agree with, so that you miss the forest because you are examining every tree so closely. The wrong way to read this book is to say that the author believes that everyone should have ten to fifteen children, if at all possible, regardless of any circumstances. In our own case, for example, my wife and I were blessed with three children, and desired to have more. The fourth child miscarried. By that time, my wife was near the end of her childbearing years, and we had to ask ourselves this question: should we continue to try to have children when my wife's migraine headaches continued to get more severe and more frequent with each pregnancy? We finally settled on a middle approach in those last few years of possible pregnancy: we wouldn't use any artificial means to prevent pregnancy, but also wouldn't strive to achieve pregnancy either for the sake of my wife's health dangers and complications. In other words, we would have loved to have had more children, if that had been God's will for us, but we also had to bow under His sovereignty in this matter. I don't believe for a moment that Judge Hekman would condemn us for this approach, given the severity of my wife's migraines. The question in such cases is this: *are you limiting your family size because you want to live selfishly to achieve your own goals or are you bowing under God's sovereignty and acquiescing with His will to limit your family size due to compelling circumstances?*

The right way to read this book is to talk to yourself like this: "I don't need to agree with every detail that the author writes to get the major takeaway from his book: will I, or will I not, let Christ be Lord also of this important area of my life that we call childbearing? *Will I continue to follow the world's way of childbearing, namely, that my spouse and I will try to achieve pregnancy only as often as we feel like it, and have only as many children as we want, or will we bow before God's sovereign lordship, and have as many children as He provides us if there are no compelling extenuating circumstances that prevent us from trying to have additional children?*" Letting that question sink in is the right way to read this book.

This is a book that needed to be written. Too many Christians today view children as something that gets in the way of what they desire out of life, so they end up living selfishly by striving to limit the number of children they bear to coincide with their all-too-frequently selfish plans. Too many Christians also fail to grasp the beauty and the joy of a large Christian family—if the Lord sovereignly provides for His own honor and glory!

By the Lord's sovereign grace, let me illustrate from my extended family. I have two brothers and two sisters. They are all God-fearing and all have God-fearing spouses, and they all have blessed marriages. My brothers and their wives have 13 and 5 children respectively, and my sisters and their husbands have 9 and 5 children respectively. My mother, who was an only child and became a remarkable prayer-warrior for her family, died seven years ago at the age of 92. When she died, she had 92 great-grandchildren (as well as 5 children, 35 grandchildren, and 1 great-great grandchild)! (Our God-fearing father died on the pulpit while leading a church service nearly three decades ago.) Nearly all of the grandchildren, by God's amazing grace, are now walking with the Lord, as are many of the great-grandchildren. My parents' prayers at the throne of grace are still being answered today! I cannot put into words for you the beauty and joy of being part of a large Christian family that fears the Lord in spirit and in truth.

So please, do not read this book wrongly; Judge Hekman is not just trying to put you on a guilt trip. But read this book rightly. Get on your knees before the face of God, and let Him be the Lord of your family size. Let your prayer be, "Lord, not my will, but Thy will be done!" In fact, let Him be the Lord of every area of your life. Surrender all to Him. Live by the maxim of Martin Luther, "Letting God be God is more than half of all true religion," and you will also taste the beauty and joy of genuine Christian living which yields all honor to the sovereign lordship of our amazing Savior who now sits at the Father's right hand as victorious Prophet, Priest, and King, and is coming again soon on the clouds to bring all His numberless children home into the eternal family of God in heaven. Then, heaven, which is as Jonathan Edwards said, "a world of perfect love," will render perfect glory forever to the Lamb who sits on the throne and through Him to the triune God forever and ever. Do you belong to this blessed, eternally joyful family and long to be in this perfect and large family forever? Bend the knee before King Jesus, repent of your sin, and believe in Christ alone for salvation (Acts 16:29–31).

—Joel R. Beeke

ACKNOWLEDGMENTS

I am so grateful to God for joining Marcia and me together in marriage over fifty years ago. Anyone who knows Marcia agrees she is truly an amazing person. Not only is she beautiful and a true helpmeet for me, but God also uses her to touch many other lives as well. Marcia's spiritual gifting is evangelism. Thank you, Lord, for my awesome wife!

But about the subject of this book, Marcia was the one who, after we had four lovely daughters and I was of the mind that four kids were "plenty," prayed that dangerous prayer: "Lord, if you want us to be open for more children, please change Randy's heart." God answered that prayer in a huge way, and I will be eternally grateful He did! Because now that I know these precious children—each uniquely crafted in His image—I can't imagine how impoverished I (and many others in this world) would be were they not here among us.

Part One

NEARLY MISSING THE TREASURE!

CHAPTER 1

Where Would My Children Be?

"Where would my children be if I insisted on being my own boss and deciding how many children to have?" This is a question I've asked myself many times. Face it, before your children are born, you don't really know what you are missing. But once you get to know their unique personalities, you don't want to lose them. *Not ever*!

Continuing my self-talk, I added, "Where would David and Suzanne and John and Scott and Laurie and Daniel and Angela and Nathan be if Jesus didn't do a miracle in my life?" You see, not too many years before—when we only had four children—I was ready to call it quits. I was looking for a compelling reason to justify putting an end to our childbearing and "get on with life." It's not that our oldest four children were a problem. Far from it! Michelle, Renee, Alicia, and Marianne are super special! While my wife Marcia's labors and deliveries for these four were far from pleasant for her, the girls were a true delight to both of us. We were so proud of them. They were respectful, intelligent, talented, cute, funny, huggable, and kissable. While not perfect, they came very close to perfection for us. We loved them a ton. But four children these days is a big family! Each child was born about two years apart, more or less fitting into our plans as we attempted to space our children with the use of birth control devices.

So there we were. Like tens of thousands of other Christian families, we were rapidly approaching what I thought should be the end of our childbearing years. It's not that we were seeking to avoid

God's will for our lives. On the contrary, we had been seeking His will for our lives since our college days. Fact of the matter was, we really didn't think God cared about our family size. We figured it was all up to us.

Marcia and I had met during college days over summer vacation, when each of us separately did a stint at the Campus Crusade for Christ headquarters in Arrowhead Springs, California. I was attending a one-week session to learn more about my responsibilities for the coming year at my Boston area campus of M.I.T. Marcia, an education major at Northern Illinois University, was at Arrowhead Springs for the entire summer. We didn't know each other at the time.

I had just broken up with a succession of college girlfriends (none of them were serious relationships), and was literally overwhelmed by the sheer number of attractive Christian coeds attending the sessions at Arrowhead Springs. I found myself wondering if, in this large cadre of Christ-following young women, God had "the one" in mind for me.

After a few days, I grabbed hold of myself and said, "Look, you came all the way from Chicago (where I was living) to Los Angeles to learn more about the Lord and sharing your faith in Christ. Are you going to waste all of your time looking for the perfect wife, or are you going to live for God?" For the first time I can ever recall doing this, I sincerely gave this area of life over to God. I told Him something like this: "Lord, I leave it up to you whether or not I will ever get married. I'm willing to be single the rest of my life if that is your choice. I simply want to grow stronger as a Christian, and not waste my time being preoccupied with a frantic search for a wife, unless that is your choice for me."

God is amazing: on the very afternoon of the day I prayed this simple prayer, I walked into the Crusade bookstore and saw this lovely young woman shopping there. Without sufficient time to scheme, and certainly having neither the reputation nor the innate ability to come up with a world class "pickup line," I nonetheless found myself talking out loud in front of the postcard rack. "I wonder what kind of postcard my mother would like." It was my hope that this young woman would hear my plaintive cry and come to my "rescue." Providentially, she responded and picked out her favorite postcard. "This is a nice card," she said innocently. For some reason (I later learned, to her chagrin), I actually bought a different card. Be that as it may, I doubt my mother ever actually saw either card. Sorry, Mom!

Our small talk soon led me to ask the young woman (whose name turned out to be Marcia) to join me for the meeting that was scheduled for that evening. This sort of "speed dating" was pretty common at Arrowhead Springs. I later learned that Marcia was not all that interested in me at that point; I, on the other hand, was eager with anticipation. After the meeting, Marcia and I met at a snack shop and talked over a coke. While I admired her blue eyes and long blond hair, what really impressed me was the sincerity of her words. "Don't you just love Jesus?" she asked with genuine wonder and awe. While I answered in the affirmative, I inwardly doubted whether my ardor for the Lord equaled what I was seeing in her. The evening's activities went like a blur. Soon I was saying goodbye, but I wanted to see her more. I asked if we might be able to meet the next evening for the scheduled *Athletes In Action* basketball game. She said that could work, then turned and walked away.

As I walked to my room, I felt as though I was floating on air. My spirit literally soared heavenward. I had never felt so excited to meet someone in all my life. She was so Christ-like, so special, so wonderful. As I crawled into bed, I thanked God I had met Marcia. I chuckled as I reflected on my prayer earlier in the day, giving over to God my marriage plans. Maybe she really *was* the one! How could anyone else on earth make my spirit so exuberant?

The next day, I could barely wait for the basketball game to begin. Arriving at the gym, I glanced at my watch, impatiently wondering when Marcia would show up. Unknown to me, Marcia had a last minute change of plans preventing her from attending the game. She attempted to send a message via other friends, but it never reached me. I continued to pace, frantically looking around the large crowd. Where was she? Didn't she care? Hadn't she felt the same special feeling I had the night before? Could she have forgotten about me so soon?

I looked again at my watch. It was time for me to leave for the airport on a commuter helicopter. I love to fly, and this was to be my very first helicopter ride. Under normal conditions, I would have been excited at the opportunity. Instead, with my spirit sagging, I climbed on board the chopper, found my seat, and barely looked outside the window as we headed to LAX. I had been *so close* to finding my true love! I didn't even get to know her last name, address, or phone number. What could I do?

It was always depressing for me to leave home at the end of a summer and travel by plane back to Boston and the rigors of M.I.T. But this year was particularly painful. I simply could not get Marcia out of my mind. Her face, her person, but especially her heart and spirit overwhelmed me. Maybe you've had this experience too. Everywhere I would go, I would often see a young woman from a distance with long blond hair and wish it was her, but knowing it couldn't be. Deep down, I knew the real Marcia was really back somewhere in Illinois, probably not even caring that someone miles away wanted to see her again. My heart was sick.

I did have a glimmer of hope—but it was slim. Prior to boarding my helicopter, I had hurriedly scratched my name and address down on a slip of paper and gave it to someone with the instructions of getting it to "a girl named Marcia who is here all summer." But our wise God was obviously in all this. My message actually made it into the hands of Marcia, who tucked it away in her suitcase. Weeks later, after returning to her campus at DeKalb, she came across this slip of paper and, almost on a lark, wrote me a short letter. Meanwhile, I had been frantically asking every Campus Crusade staff person I could find in the Boston area whether they knew this girl named Marcia who was at Arrowhead the summer before. Finally, one of the staff members came back with the information I had been seeking. I had her full name and address. But would she have any interest in me?

Not knowing if she would even remember me, I wasn't sure what to write in a letter to her. As I spent a couple of days thinking about this, Marcia's letter arrived at my fraternity! My hands trembled as I opened the blue and white envelope with a gold cross sticker on the back. My heart leaped for joy as I read:

> *September 12, 1967*
>
> *Dear Randy,*
>
> *I feel sort of funny writing to you because by now you may not remember me. However, today I started thinking about our visit at Arrowhead, and I think the Lord wanted me to write....*
>
> *I still can hardly believe that my summer was for real. It was almost like experiencing a taste of heaven. Our Father has certainly given us some great brothers and sisters, and He loves each one of us so **very** much!*
>
> *If you want to write, I would really enjoy hearing from you. Sorry I couldn't make it to the basketball game, but our dinner got a little "involved" that night.*
>
> *Because He lives,*
> *Marcia Bealer*

Did I *ever* want to write her back! The same day, I responded as follows:

> *Sept. 16, 1967*
>
> *Dear Marcia,*
>
> *Thank you for your letter; it came at the right time. I've wanted to write you for a long time but never had both your name and address at the same time. In any case, Marcia, your letter reminded me that our Father does love us....*
>
> *We talked about "the Lord shall give you the desires of your heart." I learned so much those two hours we were together that it is my desire to get to know you better. You and I are in the Lord's hands, so I am confident that my desires are His.*
>
> *Love,*
> *Randy*

And so began our courtship, largely facilitated by the U. S. Postal Service.

Surprisingly, in marked contrast to the excitement of our first meeting at Arrowhead Springs, for a period of time, our subsequent get-togethers on vacations were somewhat disappointing to me. Yet I couldn't get Marcia out of my mind and heart. I distinctly remember a time during our dating while sitting next to Marcia in a church service when, seemingly out of nowhere, it was as if the Lord was saying to me, "Just as I am one with you, so you shall be one with Marcia." That unforgettable moment made me both elated and a bit scared!

One of the most exciting times in our growing relationship occurred when I visited Marcia in January of 1969 at Northern Illinois University. It was bitterly cold and blustery outside as we walked together to her classes. But, almost like a heart transplant, God Almighty instilled in me a genuine love for Marcia that has endured through thick and thin ever since. This love is like an impenetrable, unshakable rock that has withstood the test of time and trials. I do not know how anyone can stay married without God's infinite, limitless love as a free gift of His grace. To me, it is easily worth the price of admission to Christianity merely to have that kind of love for your mate. I believe that anyone who truly asks, believes, and obeys can have it. God is more committed to our marriages than we are. At any rate, Marcia and I were married in her home town of Fenton, Illinois on June 14, 1969. The wedding was fine, but far more importantly, the marriage has been super!

At M.I.T., I had been in the Navy ROTC program, and by God's grace, I was assigned duty in the Pentagon in Washington, D.C. So that's where we began our married life together. For our honeymoon, we had planned to spend a few days in historic Williamsburg, Virginia. But after using our meager savings to buy household goods (like ironing boards, silverware, pots and pans), we had no money left for travel. So our "honeymoon" began rather ingloriously in an unfurnished apartment, made even more spartan by the fact that the moving company was two weeks late in delivering our furniture!

For those two weeks, we slept on cheap thin mats on the hardwood floor. Our table consisted of a long ironing board box supported by two other boxes. What a life! How happy we were when the *real* furniture finally arrived. As the moving van people set up our king-sized bed, newlywed Marcia raised a few eyebrows with her understandably gleeful expression, "Oh, great, a bed!"

God graciously provided a job for Marcia teaching business subjects at a local high school (Thomas Jefferson in Fairfax County) while I was engaged in computer policy management for the Navy at the Pentagon. Adjusting to all these changes was challenging, but we were so aware of God's help. Many times during that first year (and periodically since then), we have reached times of impasse in our relationship. At those moments, rather than going off in disgust, or doing something even more destructive, we prayed that God would love the other partner through us and solve the problem in His own way. Every time we humbly approached God in this way—and I do mean *every* time—we have experienced God's merciful hand of help.

While Marcia was employed as a teacher during the first two years of our marriage, she made it clear that she would much prefer getting pregnant instead. To me, it made more sense to delay children for a while to help us get our feet on the ground. Prior to our marriage, we gave very little thought to how large a family we should have. I figured we would copy our own parents' choices by having three (Marcia had two sisters and no brothers) or four (I had three sisters and also no brothers) children, but I didn't feel strongly about it at all. I simply told Marcia she should probably get on the birth control pill since we *obviously* didn't want her to get pregnant right away. I sincerely felt the issue of how many children to have was our decision. I didn't even think to pray about it.

If you had told me then that in twenty-four short years I would be the proud father of twelve children, I would not have believed you, nor would I have been eager for that to happen. But that is part of the amazing work God did in changing my heart in this area. And now that we have these infinitely valuable children, I shudder to think how impoverished we (and our world) would be if we never had the privilege of bearing them, knowing them, loving them, raising them, and eventually releasing them to God's call on their lives.

CHAPTER 2

God Shines His Truth Into My Heart

In Marcia's second year of teaching, we decided to have her quit taking birth control pills. A few months later, she began to show signs of pregnancy. We were both ecstatic. Nine months later, appropriately on *Labor* Day in 1971, Marcia gave birth to precious Michelle. I was the proudest man in Washington, D.C. "I have the best wife and best daughter in the whole world," I kept saying to myself. Perhaps new fathers can be excused for their over-the-top pride.

For inexperienced parents, everything about that first child is a momentous occasion: from sleeping, to feeding, to bathing, to burping, and to changing diapers. And Marcia—who as a child loved to play with dolls—caught on quickly. Our little sweetheart Michelle grew rapidly. Soon she was smiling and cooing back at us. What a delight she was and continues to be. Michelle is now forty-seven years old, a much-loved high school math teacher and wife of a former state legislator in Kansas who is now in non-profit work. Due to serious complications in the births of her children, Michelle has been forced to limit her child-bearing to a son and daughter—great grandkids!

For some reason, Marcia and I didn't feel right about continuing on the pill for contraception after the birth of Michelle. We talked with the Navy physicians about other means and became acquainted with the diaphragm. Prior to our marital times together, the most unromantic question would inevitably be, "Did you put that thing in?" We accepted this duty as a part of modern day marital responsibility. I didn't think for a moment at the time that such action might have spiritual repercussions. At some point we decided Marcia was ready for another pregnancy. Renee was conceived while I was still in the Navy in Washington. I left the Navy in June 1972, but we remained in Washington for a few more months to complete my law degree at George Washington University, where I had been attending as a law student in the evenings.

That fall, we moved to Grand Rapids, Michigan, where I began work in the Prosecuting Attorney's office by day, and cramming for the Michigan bar exam at night. Transition from Washington and Navy life was hard, but we survived. In December, I received word that I had passed the bar exam, for which I was most grateful.

On February 1, 1973, delicate Renee was born, after one of Marcia's easiest labors and deliveries. I'll never forget how tiny and frail Renee looked with her cute nose temporarily flattened by the birth process. Little could I guess that, in a few years time, this little bundle would grow into a young lady who could captivate audiences with her piano playing. She ultimately graduated with a Piano Performance degree from Indiana University. Renee and her husband, Luke, are parents of four amazing children and now live in Waynesville, North Carolina. Michelle and Renee became good friends from the start, with a minimum of competition. I give much credit to the bigness of Michelle's heart for that. We did our best to help Michelle understand that Renee was *her* baby too.

What amazes all parents who have more than one child is how different each is. Michelle is a very determined, sweet, and sincere person. However, as a young child, she had a tendency to have the occasional temper tantrum for no apparent reason. Renee never had tantrums, but would often fall forward on her face with seeming passive resignation when things didn't go her way.

Discipline of young children is a puzzle and concern to most new parents. The issue doesn't really come up until your child is about one year old. Then your sweet young thing wakes up one day a different person. He or she was born a sinner, and it soon becomes all too obvious. Discipline of children is not fun, but it is necessary if we want our progeny to become self-disciplined.

I enjoyed my job as an Assistant Prosecuting Attorney for our county, a position I held from 1972 through 1974. In that role, I presented cases on behalf of the State of Michigan in various county courts including Juvenile Court. While Juvenile Court had many positives, I was not impressed with the manner in which the court responded to serious juvenile offenders. In short, due to the court's excessive lenience, juvenile crime was out of control in our county, yet the court seemed determined to continue its approach. Even repeat offenders were sent back home time and again with little or no punishment.

My suggestion that the court tighten up its response to juvenile crime went unheeded. So I prayerfully considered running for the job of Juvenile Court Judge in 1974 against a well-loved incumbent. To attempt this at the young age of twenty-six was virtually unheard of, but both Marcia and I believed it to be the right decision. My approach throughout the campaign was to tell the voters to vote for me if they wanted to change the juvenile court, but vote for my otherwise honorable opponent if they didn't want to change the court. God provided the funds for the campaign and helped create much free publicity through helpful news coverage.

During this busy campaign, Marcia was pregnant with child number three, who turned out to be our third daughter, Alicia. November 5, 1974 will always stand out in my mind as an exciting day. We cast our votes that morning and gathered at my campaign manager's house that evening with friends and supporters. How exciting to see the vote totals come in with nearly 55% of the vote coming my way! What a miracle! Three days later, an even greater miracle occurred: Marcia went into labor and gave birth to our third daughter, Alicia.

I have often said that you can tell much about someone's personality from the very beginning. That was certainly true with Alicia. After her birth, the nurse wrapped Alicia up and put her under a warming lamp for a brief time. From my observations, Alicia was not happy about this turn of events! Perhaps she preferred life inside Marcia's womb to life out in our cold, noisy world. Newborn Alicia cried angrily from the other side of the room. I remember saying to Marcia and the medical personnel, "She's mad!"

I was right. There was little doubt that Alicia would clearly fall into the category of "strong-willed." During the first year of her life, she was often extremely upset with her environment. I'll never forget the time her pacifier broke in half so that it had to be thrown away. She was miserable without that comfortable mouthpiece! Fortunately, we were soon able to find another identical model. However, it apparently didn't have the same feel and taste as the one we had to throw away, so she would repeatedly spit it out and howl. The only way to get her to settle down for the next few nights was for me to rock her until she cried herself to sleep.

Because of her strong will, Alicia is a born leader. She has an incredible ability to inspire people (including myself) to do or not to do things. She is a speedy worker and usually has a lot of fun wherever she is. But it was a challenge for her (and her parents!) to come to the point where she really believed that God knows better than she does. Strong-willed people have the innate belief that whatever they are doing is right simply because they are the ones doing it.

I can still remember the occasional times we were planning as a family to go on a picnic or some other outing, but needed to cancel our plans due to inclement weather. Alicia (who was always eager to go on *any* trip) would get so angry at God and argue with Him about His (obviously) flawed decision to make it rain! Then there was the time chicken pox was making its rounds through our family. Typically, a child would be home-bound for about one week until the pox would scab over, indicating they were no longer contagious. But through her determination, Alicia found a way to vanquish the disease in less than three days. We were all surprised. She wasn't!

Along the way, Alicia entered a contest with Focus on the Family describing why she and her mother should be the lucky people to win free hair and cosmetic "makeovers." Thousands of entries poured in from all over the country. Alicia felt her usual confidence that she would win. She even put off getting her hair cut because she *knew* she was about to win the contest and have it done for free. Of course, she *did* win! Again, everyone except Alicia seemed surprised. Strong-willed kids are truly amazing! Now as an adult, Alicia is married to Simon, a pastor, and together they have five children. She is also a gifted teacher and continues to do so much with the heart and will that God has endowed her with.

In marked contrast to Alicia, but equally awesome in her own way, is daughter #4, Marianne Christine, born June 13, 1976. As strong-willed as Alicia is, Marianne is nearly the opposite: sweet, accommodating, and usually pleasant—especially when she has Jesus as her "boss." I should point out that Marcia's pregnancy with Marianne was a total surprise. The timing of her conception was totally of God. But we are so glad God made her! While Alicia expressed significant dissatisfaction immediately after her birth, Marianne, on the other hand, seemed almost to say, "Hello, wonderful world. What a nice place to nap! Oh, do you want me to cry? O.K. Here goes. Whhhaaaaa. Was that good enough?"

Don't get me wrong, Mari is by no means a pushover. But she remains incredibly merciful and kind. Even as a child, Mari would secretly give money or other valuable gifts to people who were in need. I'll never forget the time she spent about $50 of her own money on a sister who thought nobody liked her. "Why did you do this?" asked the sister, questioning Mari's motives. "Because I love you," answered Mari sincerely. She reminds me of the Mary in Scripture who anointed Jesus with expensive perfume before His death. Mari is now married and has four wonderful children of her own. I truly love this girl!

The first four children came seemingly one right after the other. It's almost like Marcia and I were married and woke up a short time later to find ourselves surrounded by four precious daughters. Now what to do? For me, four children was *more* than enough children. Not that I regretted having *any* of them. Each girl was incredible in her own way. But our house was reaching its limits, as was our car. I also felt our budget was getting stretched, and I sincerely wondered if either Marcia or I had the emotional and physical energy to have more kids. Certainly we needed to put an end to this process.

In addition to these concerns about being able to handle more children, I also had a hidden dream that would be shattered if we had more children. My hobby is flying private airplanes. My secret dream had been to own an airplane someday and fly my family around the country in it for fun. There are many four and six passenger, single-engine airplanes I possibly could purchase, but anything larger would be virtually out of the question. Plus, what would other relatives and friends say if we had another child? Having five kids was weird, and I didn't want to be thought of as weird. Marcia knew my thinking too. Yet as she listened to the desires of her heart, Marcia honestly felt she wanted another baby. So she prayed a very dangerous but, in retrospect, one of the most important prayers of our marriage: "Lord, four children is probably enough. But if you want us to have more, please change Randy's heart and mind." After praying that, little-by-little my perspective began to change. I was struck by how many Old Testament passages speak of God opening and closing the wombs of married women. (For example, see Gen. 25:21; 29:31–35; 30:17; 30:22–23; Deut. 28:4, 11, 18, 41, 62, 63; and 1 Sam. 1:5, 19–20; 2:21). God showed me that He has a much greater role in the creation of children than I had previously thought. For the first time in my life, it occurred to me how eternally important is the decision (that couples cavalierly make) about how many children to have. I came to see that this decision has a significant impact, not only on us as parents, but also on the other children in our family, and ultimately, on the history of the world, and the composition of God's eternal kingdom! It's huge!

Since high school days, I have been taught that we need to daily ensure that Jesus Christ is Lord, or boss, of all the areas of our lives. But I have yet to hear a sermon on the need to dedicate the *reproductive parts* of our lives to the Lord. Have you? Is God not sovereign in deciding who will be conceived and born? Or was it merely coincidental that Moses was born a male and specially chosen by God to become a special leader of the Israelis? Was it mere biological chance that David was the eighth born in Jesse's family and that God chose him to become an outstanding king? How about the special roles in the history of Israel played by Esther and Ruth? Obviously God wanted these people to be the gender they were and to have the personalities they each possessed. Or was that only true in biblical days? Have biological science's statistical probability and human choice now replaced God's sovereignty in our sophisticated age?

As God led me through these and other thoughts, I was soon overwhelmed by the realization that I had been wrongly controlling an area of my life that properly belonged in God's hands. Yet, at the same time, I was *petrified* at the idea of turning this reproductive area over to Him for fear that we would have another child, which, to my way of thinking, was more than we could handle. I struggled with this dilemma for a period of time, resisting God's grace because of my fear. It was around this time that I experienced an uncomfortable episode with a urinary tract infection. I felt maybe God was using this to encourage me to obtain a vasectomy to "kill two birds with one stone." The doctor dashed my hopes by saying that a vasectomy would not at all eliminate the problem; in fact, he encouraged regular relations with my wife as a way to keep the problem at bay.

Failing to resolve the issue this way, and beginning to be convicted by God on the subject, I announced to Marcia one night that we were going to trust God with whether or not we had more children. We were going "cold turkey." Marcia was ecstatic. I was a basket case. My only consolation in all this was my belief in God's attributes. I knew that He loves us and knows what is best for us. He obviously could see that, in our day and age, more than four children would be very difficult, especially for our family. I was almost 100 percent convinced that God, in His mercy, would sovereignly close Marcia's womb. We would be obeying God, and I would obtain what I knew would be best for us: no more children. Fortunately for all of us, God merely smiled at my rationalizations and did what He knew would be the best.

In a few months, Marcia's prayers for another child were answered. One evening, Marcia told me as we were getting ready for bed, "You know, Randy, my stomach doesn't feel so good, and I am a bit light-headed." Knowing as I do that Marcia hates any form of actual sickness, the smile on her face as she spoke these words confirmed my worst fears: she was pregnant again! I was going to be the father of five children! What on earth had we done? "Randy, aren't you happy?" she asked me. "Oh, sure!" I said, trying my best to sound excited. In reality, I was in emotional pain as I pondered what this all meant. Marcia could read my true thoughts and was hurt that I was not sharing her joy. Try as I might to feel happy about the situation, I failed miserably. In fact, I was in an emotional daze for about two weeks. Only as I trusted the sovereignty of God and in His perspective—that children are of infinite value—was I able to pull out of my funk. Somehow, I reasoned, everything was going to be okay. The response of friends and relatives to the news was predictably lukewarm. I really didn't know how to answer those who asked, "Is this child planned?" I wasn't strong enough yet in my new thinking to expound on the fact that, "Yes, God planned this child from before the foundation of the world." Instead, I would mutter, somewhat sheepishly, "Of course."

September 23, 1978 came soon enough, and we found ourselves again at the OB/GYN floor of a local hospital with Marcia delivering baby number five. Having had four girls up to this point, Marcia and I agreed that we really liked girls and would be pleased as punch to have another (and it would certainly save money on new clothing!). Even though ultrasounds were available then to tell you the gender of your next child, we didn't avail ourselves of this technology.

So as the big baby came out into the world, Dr. Louis Helder, a dear friend, gave the official pronouncement as soon as he could tell what it was. "It's a...boy!" he said excitedly. Marcia, unable to view the actual evidence from her vantage point, said, "There must be some mistake. We don't have boys!" She was not joking. In my family of origin, I am the only male surrounded by three sisters. Marcia has two sisters and no brothers. Her oldest sister has four daughters and no sons, and her younger sister (at that time) had no children. It honestly took more than a short discussion to convince Marcia that David was indeed "David" and not "Diane." Weighing in at almost ten pounds, dear David was a precious baby to all of us. A day or so after David's birth, our pastor made the public announcement in the Sunday morning service of our large church. "The Hekmans had a baby born, and it's a…boy!" The congregation erupted in spontaneous applause. "Didn't I tell you," I said to myself with a growing sense of pride, "that we should have a fifth child?" Yes, I plead guilty to hypocrisy.

For the most part, David was a joy to raise. He was a very kind, helpful, and hardworking young man. But occasionally as a young child, David would dig his feet in and totally refuse to do what we would ask him to do. The threat of discipline seemingly only made him more stubborn in his oppositional resolve. Finally, after a time of reflection he would agree to submit to our authority. But until he made this choice, David could be as resolute as the Rock of Gibraltar. The bottom line to me is that David represents the first fruits of my renewed thinking about a godly approach to the begetting and bearing of children. Humanly speaking, David literally would not be in this world if I had continued to control this area of my life. When I look at David, who is now a professor of management at the University of Colorado and the father of three children, I cannot help but think how impoverished I would be to never know him. Like all of his siblings, I love him! And what about those people he impacts in this world, people I will personally never meet? What if he were never born? This is beginning to sound like the storyline of "It's a Wonderful Life."

I rest in the truth that my love relationship with my wife and all of our children will go on throughout all eternity. And to think that I came so close to missing out on so many of these precious relationships! Thank you, God, for listening to my wife, and for giving me what I *really* wanted, even though I didn't know it at the time!

Let me tell you a little more about David. David has an amazing ability to save money. We have found that some of our children earn money easily and spend it as fast as they earn it, and others have an ability to save it. David, at age eleven, had already purchased a Certificate of Deposit at a local bank with money he had earned around the house. He also loves to give money to projects that need help. Frankly, he puts me to shame with his financial discipline. Thanks so much, Lord, for creating him and bringing him into our world!

CHAPTER 3

The Rest of the Crew

After "breaking the ice" with David, I found it progressively easier to welcome each subsequent child into our home. Marcia's pregnancy with our sixth child, sweet Suzanne, did not cause quite the stir in me and others that David brought (though I must confess I needed a few days to "adjust" to the news). Before I describe how special Suzie is, let me say that I actually feel guilty describing what I like about each child for fear that the other children will read something into my descriptions. I don't want them to compare themselves with each other; I want each to be the way God made them to be. I honestly love each of them with the same quantity of love (since the real love is a gift from God), but I love them in different ways because they are different people.

At any rate, Suzie is one of those children who could easily spoil her parents and fool them into thinking they have the parenting game mastered. I remember spanking Suzie a few times when she was around two years old, and a half dozen or so times since then, but that was it. When a job needed doing, it seems all we had to do was *think* about the need out loud and Suzie was already pitching in. That's not to say Suzie doesn't know who she is or that she has a poor image of herself. She is probably one of the most consistently happy people in our home, mostly because she has quickly learned to do what is right, including showing many kindnesses to others. It is not an overstatement to say that all those who know Suzanne—whether in our family or outside—have a warm spot in their hearts for her.

In 1990, our local church hosted a Christmas cantata featuring our children. Suzie played the part of a little lamb, whose greatest strength was her love, kindness, and loyalty to her Good Shepherd. While other sheep in the script played the role of being better looking, smarter, and more talented, Suzie was simply good and kind. After hearing the other sheep brag about how they were the best, and therefore should be selected to travel to Bethlehem to see the Christ-child, Suzie sang a solo that dragged tears out of the hardest-boiled church-goer. "I could give Him love," she sang. It was vintage Suzie all the way! Suzie was valedictorian of her high school class, graduated from college, and was a teacher for several years. She is now married to her husband, Andy. They have three sweet children and are very open for more.

After Suzanne came dear John Michael, our seventh-born. I should probably say at this point that in our children we see four groups of four, with similarities between the groups. That is to say, child number one has some similarities in temperament and personality with both child #5 and child #9. Child #2 links up with children #6 and #10, etc. Or, to put names to the scheme, Michelle, David, and Laurie have certain tendencies in common; so do Renee, Suzanne, and Daniel; as do Alicia, John, and Angela; and Marianne, Scott, and Nathan. Don't ask me why this is, but the kids call their counterparts their "partners." As a result, John has some of the same strong-willed (and leadership) tendencies that Alicia has, along with our eleventh-born, Angela. John loves to have fun and, as a child, he would pretend to be a pirate, cowboy, soldier, or whatever he imagined. He once insisted he would grow up to be Indiana Jones. I instinctively threw cold water on that dream. I have subsequently learned never to discourage kids who say things like this. Unless what they dream for is sinful, young children need the freedom to dream to stretch their wings. God will ultimately steer them on course. John was born on his Grandpa John's birthday (September 2), and was always full of energy. He usually initiated activities for his siblings (and occasionally for the entire family). He has a great sense of humor, as well as a good sense of timing in telling us things that made us howl with laughter. We often saw John with a sketch pad in hand, drawing very accurate pictures of soldiers, pirates, and knights. His unbridled enthusiasm and ready smile made him a favorite among his friends. John continues his artistic side by running a high fashion store in New York City. He and his wife, Cece, have three awesome boys.

Scott Henry is a handsome, very special son. Born on February 29, 1984 (a leap year day), Scott's personality is as unique as his birthday. He has an extremely sensitive and tender heart, both for people and God. He is loyal to his family and has an amazing ability to make and keep friends. Scott is now married to Lydia and together they have two daughters and a son. Scott is an executive pastor at the campus of a large church in Austin, Texas.

The differences between our children have always been interesting to me. We saw it in many ways, but one notable incident was when Marcia and I were about to leave on a mini-getaway and I was trying to communicate to two-year-old John that it would be alright to stay with these friends of ours. I said something like, "Now, John, Mom and I are going to go away for about this many days," (I showed him my five fingers) "and then we are going to come home to see you again. Okay?" Without batting an eyelash, John responded, "Don't go, Dad!" I repeated my little litany and added that nice friends of ours would be staying with the children. "Don't go, Dad!" he exclaimed with rising emphasis. We went back and forth like this about a half dozen times. Finally, realizing that no matter what he said, I *was* going to leave him, John shot back words that pierced my already aching heart. "Dad, *don't come back!*" he said with absolute finality. Tell me, where do kids get their material? Scott, on the other hand, while equally distraught about our leaving on a similar trip about two years later, simply said to me, "I don't want you to go. I want you to stay home with me." I assured him that Jesus would be there with him, and that Jesus was even stronger than Dad. His little face wrinkling up, and tears forming in his big eyes, he said (with deep emotion), "But I want someone who can hug me." "Oh, my dear Scott," I said, holding him tightly with tears welling up in my own eyes. I thought about how all of us, regardless of our age, really long for a God who can be so close that we can feel the warmth of His love. Leave it to a tender child to express this truth.

Laurie Katherine was born on January 26, 1986. She was an extremely spunky girl who could never get quite enough hugs and compliments about how much you appreciate her existence. Laurie loved to play mother hen to her two younger siblings. As a child, she called almost everyone in the family her "buddy" and seemed to get a genuine "kick" out of life. After a major struggle with same-sex attraction in her early twenties, Laurie has grown into a wonderful woman of God. She is married to her great husband, Matt, and, after giving birth to two daughters, Laurie recently gave birth to a son. They have also started a ministry called "Hole in My Heart Ministries" (himhministries.com) to "equip Christ-followers with a Gospel-centered approach to sexuality." Laurie and Matt speak around the nation and are touching thousands of lives with their podcasts and writings. We are so thankful to God for reaching her by His grace and power.

Daniel Paul has been an interesting part of our family since his birth on August 29, 1988. He genuinely loves people and will talk to almost anyone about almost anything. As a child, he loved to play a bit rough at times. One of his favorite games took place when I was lying on my back on the carpet. He would come up to my side, put his arms over his head and dive across my stomach. He never seemed to get hurt with this exuberant activity but would always come up laughing and eager to do it again. Daniel is now a medical resident in Indianapolis and is married to Elise who is already in family practice as a physician. They both love the Lord Jesus and love to help people in need. We are so grateful for them both.

Next is our little Christmas Eve baby, Angela Joy, born December 24, 1990. She is a very determined and strong-willed person and began at an early age to show incredible artistic talent. She is one of the few who came back after her high school years and thanked us for being firm with her when she had rebelled against our expectations during her teen years. I love her a ton! Angela is now married to Austin and their first child will have been born by the time this book is printed! Her skill is with interior design. A few days after I witnessed Marcia giving birth to Angela I made this entry in my journal: "I am so impressed with two things: (1) How much love, sacrifice, and courage it takes for a woman to give birth to a child, and (2) how incredible it is for God to make a unique and special child outside of human sight in the space of nine months. I don't care how many times you go through this process; the feeling each time is just as strong and clear."

After we had eleven children, I felt we might as well make the number more complete by having a twelfth. I'm so grateful God answered my prayers and fashioned Nathan Timothy, born June 26, 1993. Nate has musical, acting, and mental abilities that are phenomenal. In addition, he is just a fun, sensitive person to know. Like sister Suzanne, Nate was his high school valedictorian. He is now a computer engineer working for IBM in Austin, Texas and is married to Andrea. They have recently received their first child. Both of them dearly love Jesus.

Before we go further, I sense I should say a quick word to those couples who have made seemingly irreversible decisions to have no more children (including sterilization), and who might feel overwhelmed with grief or guilt while reading this book. Let me say this:

1. Sterilization operations can be reversed. Many couples have found this option has worked for them and are now bearing additional children. There is no guarantee, however.

2. God always accepts true believers and meets us in Christ at the point of our need rather than at the point of our perfection. There is nothing that God cannot and will not do. He always asks us to take that next step of obedience, yet His love will *never* quit! Don't let Satan, the accuser of the saints, harass you mercilessly!

3. I did not write this book to put anybody on a guilt trip, but merely to point out how God has dealt with me and our

family, and to suggest what I believe are biblical principles in the area of childbearing. My sincere hope is that I might influence couples who—like me in the past—have never even thought about God's perspectives on childbearing. I believe we have been so influenced by the world's viewpoints in this important area that we typically don't give it another thought. Yet I feel we grieve the heart of God, who longs to create children in the womb for His glory, and to benefit people on this earth.

Part Two

GOD'S PERSPECTIVES ON CHILDBEARING

CHAPTER 4

Biology Is Not God

Ideas have consequences. What we believe to be true in our minds and hearts will ultimately be reflected in our words, our behavior, and our attitudes. This is certainly true in the area of childbearing. The world has developed some clear perspectives on this issue, which we Christians have absorbed almost unconsciously in recent years. Some of these perspectives are:

1. A child is merely a biological product, the result of a sexual union of a male and female, according to statistical chance.

2. We have the right to expect a vibrant sexual life without the fear of unwanted or unexpected pregnancies. Reproduction should be reserved for those very limited times when we *intend* to "make" a child.

3. As a couple evaluates whether or not to have a child, they need to consider many factors: expense, time, effort, hassle, and other priorities like work, vacation homes, and other priorities.

4. Marriage means little more than a license for two people to live together. With the aid of contraception, marriage can be fit into almost anyone's schedule and life situation.

In this and the following three chapters, let's address these ideas, one at a time. To begin with, let's evaluate the belief that children are essentially the product of biological science. It is true that scientists are increasingly discovering the intricate details of the mechanisms whereby God designed man and other created beings in the first place. The structure of the DNA molecule is absolutely fascinating and really should incline a Christian to greater awe and respect for the majesty and wisdom of God the Creator.

But with the growth of genetics, there is also the temptation to leave God out of the equation and increasingly view children as merely the biological product of combining a male sperm with a female egg. Our modern view is that whether this occurs in the act of sexual intercourse, or in a petri dish, it is of no consequence. The bottom line is that we seem to think that *man* and impersonal scientific principles are sovereign in this biological event we call conception.

There are consequences that logically flow from the belief that children are the exclusive product of a man and a woman. The first is that we begin to feel that we, rather than God, are the creators of human life. As such, my wife and I can *choose* whether or not we want to "make" one or more children in our marriage. We can choose to make many, few, or none at all. It's all up to *us*. Another consequence of this kind of thinking is the mistaken belief that since we made this child, he or she *belongs* to us. And, as with anything else we own, if we don't like it, we feel we have a right to treat it poorly.

What if I "make" a strong-willed child? Unless I am a glutton for punishment, there will be days that I will regret my choice in making that particular child. And I will let that child know I am not fond of how he or she is wired. If this were a business transaction I would want a refund! And what if I feel I have unmet sexual needs? Why shouldn't "my" child meet these needs? After all, he or she is "mine." Could this sort of thinking be, in part, the cause of the epidemic of sexual abuse in our nation today?

A few years ago, when my wife and I had "only" eight children, we traveled to another city and presented certain of these ideas to some friends, a pastor and his wife, and their church. To put it mildly, this pastor reacted very negatively to our message. He said in effect, "That's good for you, but don't impose your principles before God on other people." I was disheartened, wondering whether somehow I had gotten off track. In those dark days of confusion, both my wife and I were tempted to view our children as our own creations rather than individuals planned by our great God. Self-accusation began to pummel our brains: "*How foolish* of us to have had any children at all, much less to have eight children!" we began to tell ourselves.

I inwardly started to feel resentment toward my children for having taken so much of my precious time, money, and energy. It was not until I again searched the Scriptures, and sought God's will through fasting, prayer, and spiritual counsel, that God assured me that we *were* right on His track. I concluded that my pastor friend was objecting to our perspectives due to the choices he had made in his own life and the counsel he had given others. Once again, I began to feel the calm peacefulness, joy, and gratitude of being the father of *God's* infinitely valuable children.

I am thoroughly convinced that much of the emotional fuel for various forms of child abuse and neglect, and certainly less overt forms of child rejection, occur today because we mistakenly believe *we* biologically make—and therefore own—our children. But when viewed as unique and special creations of an infinitely wise God, each of our children becomes a multi-billion-dollar treasure who we love to cherish and nurture. He has lovingly and wisely given them to us in trust for a handful of years. What an incredible privilege! And strong-willed children are simply leaders taking their leadership too far. We need leaders in our world! Again, what a privilege to be parents of them! I dare not abuse or neglect something that belongs to God.

Another negative consequence of this biological view of a child is our growing dependence on genetic testing of children *in utero* to determine whether there are any problems or concerns, a sort of "quality control" program for our "baby production." There are already hundreds (and soon there will be thousands) of genetic tests available to screen your unborn child for inherited diseases and even whether the child has the tendency to develop cancer or heart disease later in life. The tests can also discern propensities toward schizophrenia and other emotional or mental problems.

In a few decades, it is quite possible that a parent will be able to run a complete genetic profile on his child prior to birth. As the parents nervously huddle over the computer printout, they will be confronted with the decision of whether to allow the child to be born or "pull the plug" (through abortion) and start over. Ultimately, this technology combined with *in vitro* fertilization and the likelihood of artificial wombs (reminiscent of *Brave New World*) will allow parents the ability to select what they want in a child—a kind of mail-order parenthood.[1] "In your order, please state stock number, color, size, sex, personality type, etc."

In the interim, for those parents who refuse to have a genetic workup prior to birth or wish to continue the pregnancy despite the discovery of problems will undoubtedly be required to accept full responsibility for any subsequent medical costs associated with a "defect." Medical insurance companies and financially strapped governmental entities will demand it. We need to begin to respond to these trends now by recognizing the flaws in the underlying assumptions.

The truth is *God* makes children, not we. We men and women merely cooperate with God as *He* designs and fashions the child He wants to come into being. *God* chooses which set of genes and chromosomes to unite to make you and me as unique persons created in His image. Can anyone question that God decided for you to be male or female with certain strengths and weaknesses? David speaks to God of the process:

> For you [the Hebrew is emphatic: "you and you alone"] created my inmost being; you knit me together in my mother's womb (Ps. 139:13).

> And now the LORD says, Who formed me in the womb... (Isa. 49:5).

---

1. See Geoffrey Couley, "Made to Order Babies," *Newsweek*, Winter/Spring 1990, 94 ff.

Did not He who made me in the womb make them [menservants and maidservants]? Did not the same One fashion us in the womb? (Job 31:15).

This concept of God forming us *in utero* is found throughout Scripture. Is there any doubt that God ordained great men and women of history to be born for a purpose? It is my own educated belief that some of the great leaders of the Bible were difficult children for their parents to raise. Was the occasionally feisty Apostle Paul a strong-willed child? What if he was never born? Where would we be? This is his own autobiography:

But when it pleased God, who separated me from my mother's womb and called me through His grace, to reveal His Son in me, that I might preach Him among the Gentiles, I did not immediately confer with flesh and blood... (Gal. 1:15–16).

Similarly, God made the prophet Jeremiah for a purpose. In Jeremiah 1:5, God tells Jeremiah: "Before I formed you in the womb I knew you; before you were born I sanctified you; I ordained you a prophet to the nations."

Does our infinite, all-knowing God only concern himself with great leaders? Of course not! He custom designs *all* people for His purposes. And that means you and that means me and that means our children too. It is at this level that our modern, man-centered biological orientation to life runs so counter to scriptural truth.

Has God perhaps recently relinquished control in this area because we are now so technologically sophisticated? Of course not! Despite our knowledge, no one can conceive a child apart from His work. God alone can make and sustain life. Alexander Solzhenitsyn once said, "The law of physics and physiology will never reveal the indisputable manner in which the Creator constantly, day in and day out, participates in the life of each of us, unfailingly granting us the energy of existence; when this assistance leaves us, we die." This reminds us of Paul's statement to the Athenians, "For in Him we live and move and have our being" (Acts 17:28).

Man has learned to manipulate the DNA molecular chain; he can mutate the forms of living organisms, but he cannot turn dead chemicals into living creatures. He can gather together and manipulate the elements of life—including carbon, hydrogen, oxygen, nitrogen—but he cannot make a seeing eye or a hearing ear. God alone produces life. Are our attempts at manipulating conception and birth an attack on the sovereignty of God? I fear that we challenge His sovereignty in birth just as with euthanasia we are challenging His sovereignty in death. Man wants to become the ruler of life and death.

The fact is that God remains sovereign over who is born and who dies. *He* makes all children for His own purposes and therefore owns them Himself. As Christians, we need to respect God's choices and thank Him for the children He places in our homes in His sovereign plan.

CHAPTER 5

Putting Sex in Its Proper Place

In the last chapter, we discussed the mistaken belief that we can create a child with our sexuality apart from God—virtually at will. A second faulty idea, embraced as true by virtually all of non-Christian society (and an increasing number of Christians), is the misguided belief that we can engage in sex *without* the possibility of "making" a child. In both instances, we seem to think we can dictate to God who will and will not be born into His world.

Let's face it: our culture is largely convinced that sex and reproduction are essentially two unrelated events, unless we remove the barriers and intentionally "make" a child. There is much emphasis in our age on the necessity for all mature people to be sexually well-adjusted and fulfilled. But producing a child is another matter altogether. It is felt that only in the most limited circumstances should we allow sex to result in the conception and birth of a child. As a result of this thinking, we feel that when a woman who is sexually involved unexpectedly gets pregnant, it is therefore an "accident" and the resultant child "unplanned" and often "unwanted."

The reality, however, is that God designed there to be a much closer connection between sex and reproduction than our culture generally recognizes. Sex *does* result in the conception of a child *some* of the time. Even birth control devices cannot erase this principle that He has ordained. For example, the birth control pill fails at the rate of 2.4% per year when used conscientiously by adults. For teens engaging in sex, the pill has a much higher failure rate of

12–18% per year. Condoms and other devices are even more prone to failure. Partially due to this reality, more than four out of every ten births in the U.S. occur to non-married women. The faulty notion of the "safe sex" that is offered to our young people is essentially false advertising. Even sterilizations are unable to guarantee sex without the chance of reproduction (though the failure rates are far lower than for contraceptives). We try so hard to prevent babies being conceived in our sexual practices, and yet God seems insistent on giving many of us children because that is part of His design for this universe, and consistent with His love for His creation.

When we separate the means (sexuality) from the logical end (the possibility of a precious child), and when we begin to give inordinate priority to the means, significant imbalance will result. Our modern-day culture, focusing excessively on the value of sex, has come to the point that it virtually *worships sex*. Everywhere we turn, we are literally bombarded by the unbalanced view that life somehow revolves around sexuality.

The real problem comes when we Christians, without thinking, join this trend by also viewing sex as being more important than God says it is. God never intended sex to be an end in itself, but as a *means* to two more valuable ends: (1) communication at a deep level between husband and wife, and (2) reproduction to carry on the human race until God ends history at the second coming of Christ. While sexuality is God's idea, Scripture gives much more emphasis to the importance of marriage and children than sex.

One of the most tragic consequences of our insisting on a wall between sex and reproduction and of viewing sex as more important than children is the need for abortion. When medical technology has failed to deliver a sexually satisfied life free from the burden of children, we return to technology for some kind of remedial help. Or put a different way, when children are considered unplanned or unwanted, we need to find a convenient way to pull the plug. The primary goal for those having abortions is not some bloodthirsty longing on their part to kill an unborn child God is forming in their wombs (although that is the tragic result). They just feel they aren't in a good position to bear and raise a child, so they want to do something so that a baby is no longer in their immediate future. We Christians decry their choice for abortion. And yet, let's look in the mirror. Have we also taken deliberate steps so that we can engage in sex on a long-term basis for mere pleasure without having the "burden" of bearing and raising a child?

In Matthew 5, Jesus emphasizes how hatred is the core attitude of murder and lust the core attitude of adultery (see Matt. 5:21–22, 27–28). Similarly, the love of sex and the relative demeaning of the value of children is the core attitude that feeds abortion. If true, I have had a pro-abortion attitude in my heart, and many American Christ-followers have as well. No wonder we can't eliminate abortion in America today! We are not being the salt to preserve our nation. How we would love to divide the abortion issue into those bad guys who love to kill, and us good guys who love to protect children from bloodshed. But we must probe even more deeply. The real philosophical underpinnings for abortion are not at the level of life and death (while that is certainly the result). Those who advocate for abortion see killing only as a tragic, regrettable byproduct of a greater evil they are trying to avoid: bearing and raising an "unwanted child."

Let me approach the issue from another perspective. Many different strategies have been advanced to end abortion in our nation. Most of them revolve around modifying our laws to make abortion again the crime it should be. But do you know what would be the most effective way to truly stop all abortions in our country? To change the attitudes of people! What if right now I could snap my fingers and immediately make every man and woman in America honestly believe the *truth* that bearing and raising a child, while challenging in many ways, is one of the greatest privileges given to married couples, such that childbirth again could be called a "blessed event"?

If we could change attitudes in this way, abortion would largely evaporate overnight. We could have abortion clinics on every street corner and it would make no difference. "What?" all pregnant women would say, "have an abortion and kill my precious child? Are you kidding? I can't wait to see and hold and raise this precious little boy or girl." And these women would be right!

How can we change attitudes in our nation such that abortion will largely be eradicated? The obvious answer is to start with my and your attitudes toward children. Certainly we need to oppose abortion politically, through education and in every other legitimate way possible. But we will never get abortion out of our nation until we attack it at the level of ideas in the hearts and minds of you and me and the American populace.

Another consequence of the separation of sex and reproduction is man's attempt at the converse: if it's morally acceptable to have sex without reproduction, why not reproduction without sex? Artificial insemination, surrogate parenting, "test tube" babies, and, probably soon to be, artificial wombs, all will give us babies without sex.

While allowing for freedom of conscience in certain cases in some of these areas for couples who feel the burden of infertility, in my opinion, these approaches tend to treat children as mere biological products which may lead to some of the abuses described in the last chapter. How creative of our God to establish that, in the ideal norm, a child is produced in the loving context of marital bliss! When the couple learns that through their marital ecstasy God has creatively initiated a new life, they should be doubly overjoyed: what a thrill to participate in this amazing process whereby God is designing and producing a new person to come into the world!

Let's get practical on the issue of sexuality within a Christian marriage. The way most Christian couples today handle their sexuality is much like the general population. In data from 2014, approximately 90% of Protestant and Roman Catholic "at risk for pregnancy" women use a contraceptive method. Most use a non-permanent method, but 37% rely on sterilization of themselves or their partners. For many of these couples, it appears that little prayer goes into the decision of how many children to bear. Or, if prayer is involved, our decisions are based more on our subjective feelings than on biblical principles.

At rare times during the typical marriage, when all the lights are green—when there's money in the bank, our careers are at an acceptable stage, both parties are healthy, etc.—then and only then will we be open to "making" a baby. Otherwise, we take steps to ensure we can have our sexual relationship without the fear of an accidental, inconvenient pregnancy. We need to change this perspective. Healthy married Christian couples should be open to God for the children with which He wants to bless them, the world, and His eternal kingdom.

But what if the couple is not healthy? Are birth control methods ever appropriate for the Christian? Take the extreme case of the wife in the hospital suffering from some serious ailment. Are they not indirectly "frustrating" the possibility of children by not relating sexually at that time? Of course they are, and God understands that this is acceptable. One can think of other situations less dramatic wherein the couple says to the Lord, "We would *love* to have more children, but to do so would obviously be wrong or at least not be wise at this time."

The important principle is the Lordship of Christ in this most important area. He *does* care about children. He understands what we need to grasp: that children have the potential of greatly impacting life on this planet and the ability to live forever in His kingdom. So, please tell me why we want to play God when so much is at stake! Ultimately, we all answer to God for what we do in our marriages. But shouldn't Christian couples who are healthy enough to have a sexual relationship trust God with the outcome? What does His Lordship in this area look like? For me, it was the scariest decision I have ever made. But also one of the best!

CHAPTER 6

Children: The Cream of God's Crop

The third faulty idea in our culture flows directly from the first two. Assuming children are merely an optional product of my own will plus biological principles, and factoring in the cost and pain of raising children, the obvious question becomes, "Why have any?"

If the sum and substance of my life consists only of my seventy or so years here on earth, children do *not* make sense for me as an individual. Children *are* expensive and a lot of work. And, regrettably, no child arrives at birth with a guarantee attached to his or her big toe insuring protection against parental heartache and pain. Humanly speaking, the safest course is to avoid having children altogether or at least to keep the number down to a manageable number.

But with eternity in mind, risk, pain, and expense are far less important than my heart's desire to obey God. My sacrificial deeds done during my time on earth will not lose their reward in heaven. The best example of this, of course, is Jesus Christ who willingly accepted unbelievable risks for me in leaving the perfection of heaven to come to this sin-ravaged, germ-infested planet. He endured the pain of the cross "for the joy that was set before Him" (Heb. 12:2).

Bearing and raising a child for God has its risks and costs. But the person who gives even a cup of cold water to a little one will not lose his reward. Appendix A is a beautiful statement by a valiant woman who, in 1936, courageously and faithfully confronted the childbearing issues of her day, and chose to yield her life to be used by God to bear children for Him.[1] Appendix B is a poem by a modern-day Christian woman with similar perspectives. We have been so conditioned to think of children being conceived and born for *our* plans and purposes, that this concept seems foreign to us.

The bottom line is that we Christians are called to be godly, not to live for ourselves by minimizing our exposure to statistical risk. And God loves children. So for us to be godly, we need to love children too and not love merely "in word or in tongue, but in deed and in truth" (1 John 3:18). If I claim to love children, but don't have room for them in my life, I am only fooling myself: I really *don't* love children.

Jesus's disciples apparently had trouble with their own attitudes toward children. In Mark 10, we read how they rebuked the people who were bringing little children to Jesus for His blessing. I love Jesus's response: "But when Jesus saw it, he was greatly displeased" (Mark 10:14). Seldom do we read of Jesus being upset with His disciples. Two of the other times He was impatient with them dealt with their lack of faith (see Matt. 8:26; 17:20). It *does* take faith to visualize the value of a child. Jesus, in looking at a child, sees not only a young person with wonderful qualities of innocence, loyalty, faith, and love; He also visualizes this child's future. When we try in vain to comfort a colicky baby, all we see is a screaming, noisy child. God sees a Moses, a David, a Daniel, an Esther, and a Ruth. We see the short-run; He sees a child in light of eternity. Appendix C is a great poem by Henry Wadsworth Longfellow on the value of children who keep the whole human family moving ahead.

Returning to Mark 10, Jesus, after rebuking His disciples and describing the incredible value of children, demonstrated His love for them by taking the children in His arms (I am confident with a smile on His face and joy in His heart), putting His hands on them and blessing them (v. 16). The heart and action of the Second Person

---

1. *The Banner*, July 24, 1936.

of the Trinity to take time to love children is an excellent example for us, His followers.

Elsewhere in the New Testament, Paul advised younger widows to "marry, bear children, manage the house, give no opportunity to the adversary to speak reproachfully" (1 Tim. 5:14). Is this only applicable to young widows or to all young wives? It clearly seems to be a more general exhortation. Elsewhere, Paul tells older women to "admonish the young women to love their husbands, to love their children, to be discreet, chaste, homemakers, good, obedient to their own husbands, that the word of God may not be blasphemed" (Titus 2:4–5).

Psalm 127, tells us how children are a heritage from the Lord and a reward from Him. They are like arrows in the quiver of a warrior. Psalm 128 continues this theme, describing the blessings reserved for the man who fears the Lord. Those blessings include having a tableful of children. God help us to view things from His perspective—and to realize the infinite value of every child!

CHAPTER 7

Marriage *Is* a Big Deal!

The last faulty idea we want to consider logically flows from the others. If through medical technology I can now have a vibrant sex life without an inconvenient pregnancy to disrupt my goals, marriage is not that significant an event. Practically anyone can get married today at any stage of life thanks to the help of contraception (and for many, the backup of abortion).

So many couples today (including my wife and myself) begin married life with both husband and wife working for a number of years. We even have many young women earning their husbands' ways through seminary, law school, or medical school, during which time the idea of children is put "on hold." When we finally get to the place where we can comfortably "start our family" after a significant number of years, we stop using contraception and attempt to have a child.

In the biblical norm, however, the husband is obliged to support his wife and any children God may give. First Timothy 5:8 says, "But if anyone does not provide for *his* own, and especially for those of *his* household, *he* has denied the faith and is worse than an unbeliever" (emphasis added). Proverbs 24:27 reinforces the same idea, "Prepare your outside work, make it fit for yourself in the field; and afterward build your house." Solomon's counsel is for us to get our income production going before building our homes (or our families which the Hebrew word includes). We should not allow the availability of contraception to negate this biblical principle. God views marriage as being much more significant than many of us currently consider it to be. Marriage is so basic and important to human life from God's point of view that it is even discussed in Scripture pre-fall, back in the account of Adam and Eve, "Therefore a man shall leave his father and mother and be joined to his wife, and they shall become one flesh" (Gen. 2:24). In scriptural accounts, marriage was *always* accompanied with the hope for children. Children were seen as a sign of God's blessing. Barren women were often seen pleading with God for offspring.

In addition to these numerous examples are other scriptural perspectives. In Malachi 2, for instance, God describes why He hates divorce. God was angry with His people because men were breaking faith with their wives, described as the men's "partners," the wives of their marriage covenants (v. 14). And then God tells us the reason for marriage:

> But did He not make them one, having a remnant of the Spirit? And why one? *He seeks godly offspring.* Therefore take heed to your spirit, and let none deal treacherously with the wife of his youth (Mal. 2:15, emphasis added).

Paul tells us in Ephesians 5:22–33 that human marriage is a wonderful analogy of Christ's relationship to His bride, the church. What could be more sacred or significant? Even to mention the idea of contraception in connection with this analogy trivializes and cheapens our blessed relationship with our Lord. Scripture tells us that Christ died to bring "many sons to glory" (Heb. 2:10). How wrong for the church even to consider taking steps to prevent the "new birth" of a large brood of "baby" Christians, perhaps out of our self-centered desire to avoid the hassle of having to disciple these babes into maturity.

God wants His bride to have a passion for the lost. Equally, I believe God wants marriages of His people to bear the fruit of children He ordains. Scripture makes it clear that no one is obligated to get married. If a person really does not want to consider having children, he or she should remain single. Biblical marriage is much broader and deeper than merely church-sanctioned sexual intimacy. It is an incredibly rich relationship that provides the nucleus of a new family. As such, it should include the possibility, indeed the hope, for children.

We should enter marriage with full commitment to accept our spouses unconditionally for life along with the hope for the children God may choose, in His sovereignty, to create through us. Marriage is a high and holy human relationship. Our marriage is not primarily a means to make me happy, but as with all of my life, it is designed to make me grow in conformity to Christ and in holiness, so as to give glory to God. We get joy as we live, not for ourselves, but for our Maker and Redeemer. May God help us treasure the spouses He has given us and to let our marriages give great glory to the One who instituted marriage in the first place.

Part Three

RESPONDING TO ARGUMENTS

CHAPTER 8

"Judge Put Self above the Law"

I am told the classical Jewish mind responds to God's commands with the attitude, "First, I will obey, and later I will understand *why* I obeyed." While this mentality certainly goes against the grain of our modern Western culture, probably most Christians have obeyed God with this type of attitude at some point in their lifetimes. In such situations, it is not until later—sometimes *much* later—that we can see God's wisdom in asking us to obey in the area we dutifully accepted on "blind" faith. God sees the big picture, while we often see little more than the nose in front of our faces.

One area often accepted on "blind" faith by believers is in response to the scriptural injunction to, "Count it all joy when you fall into various trials" (James 1:2). This concept of joy in the midst of pain is found throughout the New Testament: "we also glory in tribulations" (Rom. 5:3). "In everything give thanks; for this is the will of God in Christ Jesus for you" (1 Thess. 5:18). "Giving thanks always for all things to God the Father in the name of our Lord Jesus Christ" (Eph. 5:20).

I can't read these verses without thinking about a very painful time in my own life shortly after I ruled on a case involving a thirteen-year-old pregnant girl who wanted an abortion. Although she was physically mature and became pregnant through a relationship with her boyfriend, Planned Parenthood had scared her by telling her that her heart would stop if she tried to give birth.

After hearing the testimony of experts who said abortion was not in her best interest, I gave my legal opinion. In it, I ruled against abortion based on the evidence. But I felt I needed to be totally honest with my underlying beliefs. Therefore, I went out on a limb to describe how unjust it was to consider killing this prenatal life within her, solely for her own expediency. I was a Juvenile Court Judge sworn to protect *born* children from abuse and neglect. Imagine how irrational it would be for someone to think I could, at the same time, cavalierly order the brutal killing of an innocent child who just happens not to be born yet! Bottom line, I wasn't that schizophrenic! National wire services carried the story to news outlets around our entire nation. I received hundreds of letters (80% of which were positive). The news accounts, however, were generally critical. I was interviewed by scores of radio and TV outlets around the country. Even the *New York Times* got into the fray with a small editorial denouncing my decision.

Within days of the case, the pregnant girl began to wonder why everyone was making such a big deal about abortion. She requested and ultimately saw an ultrasound "picture" of her unborn boy who was about four to five months along. Once she saw her son sucking his thumb in her womb, this girl, who had been so adamant about wanting an abortion, immediately changed her mind and decided her baby must live. She even wrote me a letter thanking me for giving her time to change her mind.

Before changing her mind, however, the "spin" put on my case by the local media pitted this poor pregnant teenager—who obviously "needed" an abortion—against this uncaring, authoritarian judge with his antiquated ways. Once the girl changed her mind, however, those advocating "freedom of choice" were stuck. Since the media couldn't publicly argue the baby should be forcibly aborted, they needed to find another way to express their displeasure at the turn of events.

The method used by the *Grand Rapids Press* was to editorialize the issue, putting me directly in the line of fire. "Judge Put Self above the Law" was the headline. Believe me when I say the headline was the kindest part of the editorial. Thereafter it described how the issue in the case was not so much about abortion, as about a judge who was biased, and probably "pandering" to his political constituency.

When I first saw this editorial, I was immediately engulfed in pain as I considered how unjust the writers were to misconstrue my true motivation. In reality, I had struggled over this case with sleepless nights and much soul-searching, absolutely convinced I was putting my professional future in serious jeopardy for the sake of this baby. But I concluded that some things in life were far more important than a job. As I read the editorial, I found myself saying, "This is *so* unfair!"

But then God brought to mind the verses commanding us to say "thank you in everything." Note the verses do not say, "feel thankful," because I didn't! But I painfully decided with my will to say "thank you" to God even for this unjust insult. Once I obeyed, however, a very unexpected sense of joy came into my heart and—to my mind—a thought of what I could do. I could write a response to this editorial that they would hopefully publish!

It took me a while to write what I considered a persuasive piece. But I submitted my response to the *Press* and they published it. Even friends of mine, who were beginning to be swayed by the negative publicity about me, said my response helped bring them clarity. But I also sent a copy of my response to the hundreds of folks who wrote me from around the nation. The result was that my words were published in scores of other newspapers and periodicals (including the *San Francisco Examiner*) and in at least one book as well. So obeying God and saying "thank you" when it didn't make sense, ultimately led to my understanding later *why* I had obeyed. God always gets the last word!

Jesus Christ wants to be Lord of all areas of our lives, including the reproductive area—an area often considered "off limits" to God by many modern Christians. I am convinced, however, that when we finally decide to obey God and let Him be the Lord of even this area of our lives, while the decision may often be very scary (it certainly was for me!), we eventually will see God's wisdom in the process.

Sadly, as we haltingly begin to take our first baby steps of obedience in a new area of our lives, often well-meaning friends and relatives will begin to question our sanity—especially if it's in a subject matter they themselves don't fully understand. Like Job's "friends," they mean no harm, but can certainly cause us to doubt what God has shown us from His Word to be true.

However, the exciting thing about courageously following God is that, because God's ways are based on absolute truth, they are guaranteed to win in the long run. The familiar words from Proverbs fit well here: "Trust in the Lord with all your heart, and lean not on your own understanding; in all your ways acknowledge Him, and He shall direct your paths" (Prov. 3:5–6). In marked contrast is another Proverb, found in both 14:12 and 16:25: "There is a way that seems right to a man, but its end is the way of death." In other words, arguments which oppose God's truth may appear reasonable at first blush, but in the end have a very sad result.

In this section of the book I respond to some of the major questions people ask, and objections they raise when they consider the implications of letting God be the Lord of their family size. The questions people raise range from the simple ("Will we have enough money for more children?"), to the more complex ("Isn't our world overpopulated already?"). Because each issue is treated independently of the others, you need only read the questions that are important to your situation.

CHAPTER 9

The Financial Argument

"I can't afford another child!"

Many of you have read the book or seen the movie, *Cheaper by the Dozen*. Besides loving the title, even more I enjoy the delightful story of the zany, but totally true adventures of the Frank Galbraith family. Written by one of Frank's twelve children, *Cheaper by the Dozen* makes you envious of the non-stop activity and fun experienced by Frank's burgeoning family. But who of us really believes children are "cheaper by the dozen?" Is there any truth to this catchy phrase?

To begin with, we need to ask the obvious question: "Cheaper than what?" Twelve children are definitely not cheaper than no children at all. And—all things being equal—not cheaper than eleven children! But the *per unit* cost (if I may be so crass in speaking this way about children) does decrease the more children are added to a family. That is, each additional child costs progressively less to raise than the one before (discounting inflation, of course), resulting in a reduced average rate as the family size increases.

But let me state the obvious: Children are expensive, whether you have one or a dozen. But so is anything else that is worthwhile in life! People spend exorbitant amounts of money on various hobbies and other interests, not to mention fancy homes, cars, vacations, and wardrobes. When people say they can't afford another child, what they are really saying is that their limited resources are being devoted towards other things that they feel are more important.

Let's get more specific on the cost of children. Almost everyone has seen the perennial newspaper articles on how much it costs to raise a child from birth to age eighteen. A relatively recent article, drawing data from the U.S. Department of Agriculture, pegs the cost between $145,000 and $455,500 per child, for a family with two children and two wage earners.[1] The wide disparity between these two numbers is based on the income level of the parents, and the region in the United States where the family resides. The average overall cost per child was $245,000, and did not include the cost of college.

But the studies and articles that talk about the expense of children ignore some of the financial advantages of children from a tax standpoint. Now that our children have grown up, and are largely on their own, I really miss those exemptions!

Also, bear in mind that the "price tag" data of what it costs to raise a child from birth to age eighteen was never intended to be used to discourage a couple from bearing and raising a child. This data was originally developed to aid families in formulating a budget. More recently, it has been used by courts to calculate proper child support orders and in helping to determine wrongful death and malpractice claims. Obviously, if you have a child, no one is going to send you a monthly bill for $1134.26 (assuming a total eighteen-year cost of $245,000). You spend what you choose to spend on your child. Jesus Christ, the very Son of God, was born in a stable, and was placed in a borrowed manger as a crib. You make do with what you can afford. A child's life is much more important than whether or not his wardrobe comes from St. Laurent of Paris.

Further, even governmental data itself confirms the fact that the "official" cost information doesn't tell the whole story: Subsequent children are increasingly cheaper to raise than the first child. According to the USDA:

---

1. Melanie Hicken, "Average Cost of raising a child hits $245,000," CNN Money, August 18, 2014, http://money.cnn.com/2014/08/18/pf/child-cost/

The cost estimates of raising urban and rural non-farm children reflect average costs per child in families with not more than five children. Size-specific estimates developed for two, three, four, and five-child families indicate that total costs *per child* decrease as family size increases. Per child costs in five-child families average from 20–24 percent below those in two-child families.[2]

This stands to reason. Preparations for the first child are much more elaborate than what is needed for subsequent children. How about the long-term impact of a big family on the parents' economic well-being? Apparently the parents spend their money one way or another, since reliable studies show that there are no long-term economic disabilities for parents who have many children, compared to other adults with few or no children. "There is no difference in income or living standards among the elderly by number of children ever born."[3] In fact, I would selfishly prefer to have more children to provide some help (if needed) for my wife and me when we are older, in light of growing concerns about the long term stability of our Social Security system. (We will explore this more when we discuss the "overpopulation" issue.)

So the cost of raising children, while not insignificant, is not impossibly onerous either. And the person who is anxious about the lack of resources is probably ignoring some comforting assurances from God's Word.

Scripture is full of promises about how God will certainly meet the needs of any family or group that obeys Him. If there were no God on the throne of the universe, man would be forced to fend for himself. He would live in constant fear of extinction. But we believe that God exists and that "He is a rewarder [wage-payer] of those who diligently seek Him" (Heb. 11:6). Do we believe in a God who

2. Carolyn Edwards, "USDA Estimates of the Cost of Raising a Child: A Guide to Their Use and Interpretation," *USDA, Miscellaneous Publication 1411*, 25–26.

3. Thomas J. Espenshade, et al., "Family Size and Economic Welfare," *Family Planning Perspectives*, 15, no. 6 (November/December 1983): 294.

rules the universe? Do we really believe Jesus when He tells us that we are not to worry about food or clothes? If God feeds the birds, and clothes the grass of the field, will He not also care for us? If He sees the sparrow fall, will He be able to forget any of His people, created in His own image? I can hear someone say, "Right, but He doesn't put the worms in the birds' mouths!" No, we have to do our part, but doesn't He give us that ability? And, really, how many birds starve to death?

Throughout Scripture, the key issue is not whether I, as a person apart from God, am able to provide for my family. The real issue is whether I am in the will of God. If I seek with all my heart to obey Him in thought, word, deed, and attitude, and thereby do my part, He *will* care for me and my family. And I need not then spend time worrying about my self-preservation or the future: "But seek first the kingdom of God and His righteousness, and all these things [food and clothing] shall be added to you" (Matt. 6:33).

Let's explore some other Scriptures on this point:

Oh, that they had such a heart in them that they would fear Me and always keep all My commandments, that it might be well with them and with their children forever! (Deut. 5:29).

When all these things come upon you [these blessings and cursings]…and you call them to mind…and you return to the LORD your God and obey His voice…with all your heart and with all your soul…then the LORD your God will…prosper you and multiply you more than your fathers. And the LORD…will make you abound in all the work of your hand, in the fruit of your body, in the increase of your livestock, and in the produce of your land… (Deut. 30:1, 2, 5, 9).

Whose belly You fill with Your hidden treasure; they are satisfied with children, and leave the rest of their possession for their babes (Ps. 17:14).

The Lord is my shepherd; I shall not want (Ps. 23:1).

Behold, the eye of the LORD is on those who fear Him, On those who hope in His mercy, To deliver their soul from death, And to keep them alive in famine (Ps. 33:18–19).

The young lions lack and suffer hunger; but those who seek the LORD shall not lack any good thing (Ps. 34:10).

O LORD, You preserve man and beast (Ps. 36:6b).

I have been young, and now am old; yet I have not seen the righteous forsaken, nor his descendants begging bread. He is ever merciful, and lends; and his descendants are blessed (Ps. 37:25–26).

Praise the LORD! Blessed is the man who fears the LORD, who delights greatly in His commandments. His descendants will be mighty on earth; the generation of the upright will be blessed (Ps. 112:1–2).

That our sons may be as plants grown up in their youth; that our daughters may be as pillars, sculptured in palace style; that our barns may be full, supplying all kinds of produce; that our sheep may bring forth thousands and ten thousands in our fields…. Happy are the people who are in such a state; happy are the people whose God is the LORD! (Ps. 144:12–13, 15).

Oh, that you had heeded My commandments! Then your peace would have been like a river, and your righteousness like the waves of the sea. Your descendants also would have been like the sand, and the offspring of your body like the grains of sand; His name would not have been cut off nor destroyed from before Me" (Isa. 48:18–19).

Probably the most graphic illustration of God's provision for His people is seen in His care for them for forty years in the wilderness. Psalm 78 describes the attitude of many of the Israelites at the time:

Yes, they spoke against God: they said, "Can God prepare a table in the wilderness? Behold, He struck the rock, so that the waters gushed out, and the streams overflowed. Can He give bread also? Can He supply meat for His people?" Therefore the LORD heard this and was furious…because they did not believe in God, and did not trust in His salvation. Yet He had commanded the clouds above, and opened the doors of heaven, had rained down manna on them to eat, and given them of the bread of heaven. Men ate angels' food; He sent them food to the full (Ps. 78:19–25).

The lesson is clear: God's hand is not so short or weak that He cannot care for us.

"Well, that was then," you say. "And they were God's chosen people. But this is now, and God doesn't work that way today!" Really? Fred and Nelly Van Stralen are friends of ours from the Toronto, Canada area. We have lost recent contact with them, but a number of years ago when we visited them they had fifteen children. Even though Nelly did not work outside of the home, Fred was able to make ends meet for his large family through his income as a *mail carrier* in Canada. His family accepts a life of somewhat simple tastes. They buy bulk foods and occasionally are the recipients of donated clothing.

My family visited the Van Stralens in the summer of 1985 at their large home containing even a fun swimming pool. It was exciting to hear how they came into possession of this home—mortgage free—which Fred said was worth upwards of $300,000 at the time. The prior owner had it on his heart to sell the home to the Van Stralens merely for the cost of the land itself upon which the home stood! As Fred put it, "God literally *throws* blessings at us when we, His children, obey Him."

As the Van Stralen children have matured, they have acquired jobs using the ability to work gained in part by growing up in their family. Some of the children own horses, and the family even traveled as a group to Europe! The "fun quotient" in the Van Stralen family is very high, and trust me when I say their family lacked no amount of excitement! About one-and-a-half years after our visit, we heard that the family moved to a fifty-acre country home, allowing them ample space for their horses and other activities. Isn't God amazing!

Another large family, whom I have only "met" by reading an account in the newspaper, are the Sheptocks of New Jersey. Rudy and his wife, Joanne, have twenty-six children, seven biological ones and nineteen adopted. They live in a rambling thirteen-bedroom, seven-bathroom home in Penpack-Gladstone, New Jersey.

The Sheptocks consume more than $500 worth of groceries and do upwards of 100 loads of laundry per week. Mr. Sheptock works as a maintenance supervisor for a local public school system. In addition, publicity of the family has prompted donations. To what do the Sheptocks attribute their source of supply? Listen to Mr. Sheptock:

> We talk about God so much that people think we're nuts.... But He has always provided for us. Without God, there's no way we would ever be able to take care of so many children.

I could also share how God has amazingly met the financial needs of our own family through the years. Our most difficult year financially was 1989 when our oldest, Michelle, was a freshman at Wheaton College in Illinois. We only had ten children then, but, with our newly built twelve-bedroom house that God had provided and my decision *not* to borrow for her education, we pinched pennies pretty tightly. The next year, second-born Renee was planning to attend Indiana University and major in Music (Piano Performance). I saw no possible way to make it happen financially, so I cried out to God for help.

Then God moved me from being a trial court judge, to starting Michigan Family Forum, associated with Focus on the Family. I started commuting from our home in suburban Grand Rapids to the Lansing, Michigan area on an almost daily basis. I told Michelle to apply at Michigan State University, as it was much cheaper than Wheaton College. She dutifully complied with my request, but didn't tell Wheaton she wasn't returning.

In August of that summer before her sophomore year, friends of ours, a neat couple in our little Baptist church, heard of Michelle's circumstances. It just so happened that the husband was an attorney for a private foundation that offered scholarship money for families that were involved in ministry. Long story short: Michelle was able to return to Wheaton College that fall, and this generous foundation helped at least half of our kids go to college without any debt! The remaining kids also have been able to complete college debt-free (with only one exception—a child whose questionable choices at the time necessitated an additional year of school that he paid for). But his debt is minimal! I could go on describing how God has continued to help us in housing, in food, in clothing, in medical care, and even in dropping a fifteen-passenger van out of the sky for our needs! He has *always* wonderfully and lovingly been faithful to meet our needs!

A final thought about us. Early in our marriage, when I was earning about $7600 per year as a Naval officer in Washington, D.C., I was tithing (giving ten percent) of my *net* paycheck to our local church. A friend asked me if I wanted God to bless my net income or my gross income. I obviously wanted Him to bless all of it. He said I should tithe ten percent of the gross amount of my check! I didn't see how that was possible, but, in faith, we did it anyhow. To repeat myself: God has *always* met our needs from that point onward—regardless of how many wonderful children He has brought our way!

Bottom line, the question is not whether God is actually big enough to meet our financial needs; the real question is whether or not we will trust Him and love Him enough to obey Him. When we begin our life of faith, doing so seems far scarier than living by sight. If you offered a group of people their choice of either one million dollars in cash, or God's absolute promises in the Bible to meet their needs, most of them would probably take the cash. But how foolish! God owns everything. And He loves us dearly! How can we possibly lose with Him?

Marcia and I would much rather have another precious, unique child—created in God's image, and living in our home—than to possess more money. I tell my children *they* make me rich. Since each child is worth more than a trillion dollars, I must be one of the richest people in America! And based on the experience of many people, not only are we rich in spiritual assets with our children; it is just like God to materially bless us as well, as we trust and obey Him.

Bottom line: No true believer in Almighty God should ever use the fear of running out of money as a reason to limit his or her family size. It just doesn't add up!

CHAPTER 10

The Intelligence Argument

"If I have a larger family, my children's IQs will be lower: I'll raise a group of morons!"

Many of the arguments offered as to why big families are bad have at least an aura of plausibility surrounding them. Such is certainly true in this area of children's intelligence.

Obviously, the more children a person has, the less time he or she has to spend with each one individually. If that is true, it is fair to ask how even the most dedicated parent of a large family has time to motivate each of his or her children to realize their full mental and intellectual potential. Articles have been written which seem to confirm the idea that larger families mean lower IQ's for the children. Perhaps the seminal article on the subject, an article that is still cited today, was written forty years ago. Authored by Robert B. Zajonc of the University of Michigan, it had such a compelling title: "Dumber by the Dozen."[1]

In his article, Dr. Zajonc emphatically stresses the intellectual advantages that accrue to children from smaller families since a child's IQ seems to drop in relationship to how many siblings that child has. I find interesting, however, that twelve years after his 1975 article in *Psychology Today*, Dr. Zajonc—still obviously interested in this area—was quoted as saying he would not recommend

---

1. Robert B. Zajonc, *Psychology Today*, January 1975.

using his data for family planning decisions since "many factors are completely unknown."[2]

Another researcher, James Higgins of Michigan State University, offered a plausible explanation for Zajonc's data: "Parents of large families tend to have low IQ's, and...therefore the children's IQ's are merely a reflection of their parents' [IQ's] and are not related to the size of their families."[3] Clearly, if any one group is having large families in our day, it is not the upper class. More recently, another research report attempted to resolve the debate by stating: "Although low-IQ parents have been making large families, large families do not make low-IQ children in modern U.S. society."[4]

So even the experts are not convinced the data actually supports the hypothesis that kids come "dumber by the dozen." Clearly, there are many factors at work to produce any statistical conclusion. As they say, "Statistics never lie, but statisticians [often] do."

As we will be showing in Chapter 18, Hispanics and African Americans in the United States are having considerably more children per woman than are white women. Yet 72% of African American children and 53% of Hispanic children born in the United States are born to unmarried females. Is it possible that the lack of two parents raising their children may contribute to lower scores on IQ tests?

Then, too, just how accurate a measure of intelligence is IQ anyhow? Does a high IQ guarantee success in life, or an ability to relate to people or being a good employee, husband, wife, or parent? Of course not! As Yale psychologist Robert Sternberg says, "We've gotten so hung up on IQ that we have forgotten it isn't very predictive

---

2. "Does Smaller Family Boost Child's IQ?" *The Grand Rapids Press*, June 2, 1985.

3. "Smaller Family," *The Grand Rapids Press*, June 2, 1985.

4. Rodgers, Joseph Lee, H. Harrington Cleveland, Edwin van den Oord, and David C. Rowe, "Resolving the debate over birth order, family size, and intelligence," *American Psychologist* 55, no. 6 (June 2000): 599–612.

of life success."[5] Scholars are still spending great amounts of time and money to discover alternative methods of measuring the ability to cope with the demands of life in our culture. They feel there are fifteen to twenty-five different kinds of intelligence that people possess that are useful in living. For example, some children show great ability to understand the dynamics of interpersonal relationships in their classroom; they can tell you who feels hurt or is jealous or afraid, while other children are almost completely oblivious to such matters. Still other children, while only moderately gifted in conventional academic matters, are very gifted in encouraging other children who are emotionally distraught or at mobilizing a diverse group of peers to accomplish a task.

And many children from large families have a "built-in classroom." For example, if a child from a family of twelve children learns to get along with all eleven other unique siblings (most of the time at least!), and thereby learns to "read" other peoples' actions and attitudes fairly well, wouldn't you suppose this person would be substantially more "street smart," and have higher Emotional Intelligence (EQ), than a child from a small family? I have certainly seen this in my own children.

The mere press of numbers requires a degree of maturity and self-reliance that children from smaller families will not necessarily develop well. For example, our fifth-born, David, at age twelve, all on his own, started saving the money he would need for college. He accumulated hundreds of dollars for that purpose. He graduated near the top of his high school class, performed admirably in college and grad school, and is now a professor at the University of Colorado. Our sixth-born, Suzanne, and our twelfth-born, Nathan, were both valedictorians in their high school classes. We have raised children who have become teachers, engineers, a physician, a nurse practitioner, the manager of a high-end fashion boutique,

---

5. "New Intelligence Tests Emphasize Abilities Overlooked by IQ Exams," *Wall Street Journal*, March 12, 1987.

a musician, and an artist, who have all done exceptionally well in
school and in life, by the grace of God.

I am personally convinced that the data in this area suggesting that large families produce morons is mostly the result of the
"intelligent" upper middle class giving more priority to money
and careers than raising a large number of children. How unfortu-
nate it is when highly motivated and financially successful couples
spend their best years and energies merely on temporal success, but
ignore the incredible privilege of seeking God's power and grace
to leave a genuine legacy by raising a goodly number of world-
changing and world-blessing children. Sure, these folks will have
their "millionaire family" of a girl and a boy along the way. But
that's it. "There are many more important things for 'me' to do than
to raise another child," they say. But they are forgetting, for the most
part, that the world never has enough quality people who can lead,
love, learn, and give.

The theory that having a large family means you will be raising a pack of morons does not jibe with reality. John and Charles
Wesley of England were children number fifteen and eighteen of
a family of nineteen children, and yet their preaching and teaching helped spread revival and prevent the cancerous spread of the
French Revolution to England. Benjamin Franklin, obviously a
brilliant statesman, author, and inventor in colonial America, was
also the fifteenth born child (of a total of seventeen children).

David, the man after God's own heart, was the eighth son of
Jesse and certainly did not lack for any mental quality. He had at
least nineteen sons by his wives as well as numerous daughters. One
of his sons was Solomon, who, apart from his moral and idolatrous
indiscretions, was the wisest man who ever lived. Job had a total
of twenty children, the last ten of whom were highly regarded—
especially his beautiful daughters (see Job 42:14–15). There is
certainly no suggestion from Scripture that, for the sake of our children's intelligence, we should restrict the number of children we
have. God will always provide for the needs of the children He
forms in the womb.

But what about the need for parents to mentally stimulate their children—and help them to think, reason, read, and learn their multiplication tables? What larger families find is that often the older children assist the parents in helping to train the younger ones in behavior and skills. This nourishes the bonds of love among the children, and even helps the older children to get better at learning the subjects being taught.

In conclusion, there appears to be no significant evidence that children from larger families are less intelligent or less capable than children from smaller families. In fact, there is reason to believe that children from larger families, particularly where there are two parents, are better adjusted and more capable of flourishing in life than children from smaller families. Can't we trust that God has greater wisdom than we do in deciding how large a family we should have? Won't He give us the grace to raise those children He chooses to bless us with, be it many or few? Don't allow the fear of raising a group of unintelligent kids prompt you to arbitrarily restrict your family size. It's not smart!

CHAPTER 11

The Career Argument

> "If I have children, their care will impede me
> from pursuing the career that
> gives me a great deal of satisfaction."

Perhaps the most honest response to this objection is simply to agree with it. Since God has given us—men and women—only twenty-four hours per day, and since both children and careers consume a great amount of time and energy, it is impossible for both children and careers to be our top priority.

I have deliberately included both sexes in my statement. The temptation, of course, is to consider that only women have to wrestle with the task of trying to juggle the tension between children and career. But in reality, we men must also be willing at times to forego promotions or relocations for the sake of our children.

Society today—perhaps more than ever before—draws women away from their children and into the work force to "realize their full potential." But men are also lured away from their God-appointed role of nurturing their precious children by the enticing call of money, advancement, and status. Christians are also susceptible to this societal pressure as we see increasing numbers of Christian "workaholic" fathers and career mothers pursuing the "good life," as they deposit their infinitely precious children, day after day, at day care centers, relegating all but a fraction of the child-rearing to paid surrogates. Compounding the problem for Christians are often additional church responsibilities, which can rob children of their parents' time as well. The good is often the enemy of the best for lack of time. I'll never forget the three years I spent on the board of a fine evangelical church where innumerable meetings took me away from my young children many times a month. Shouldn't the older men in churches—the "elders"—perform the lion's share of leadership and let our younger fathers provide much needed leadership in their homes?

But let's get back to our principal issue. Let me ask this: How is it that we as a culture have lost the conviction that our children ideally need *both quality and quantity time* with their parents to grow up emotionally and spiritually healthy? Certainly, God will extend His grace to children who through circumstances—like desertion, or the death of a parent—cannot have access to that parent. God makes it clear that He is a "father to the fatherless."

But I'm afraid we try God's patience when we, as a culture—and especially Christians—demand that God makes up for our woeful lack of involvement with our children after we have selfishly decided to pursue the activities that will help us "find ourselves." The tragic truth is we often simply want to get more of this world's goods and status, often to the temporal and even eternal detriment of our precious children.

You've probably heard or read about the statistics showing that the average father spends only a handful of minutes per day directly interacting with his young children. And, in most homes, the father needs to compete with video games, social media, and other forms of entertainment that touch the heart of his children. Despite the challenges, we fathers need to understand that God expects more of us than merely putting food on the table and clothes on our children's backs. I don't know where we got off the track in our thinking that women are the sole caretakers of children. Women certainly have a role that is indispensable. But in Ephesians 6:4 we read: *"Fathers*...bring them [your children] up in the training and admonition of the Lord" (emphasis added). In Hebrews 12, we read about how loving *fathers* perform the discipline of their children. As I used to tell the fathers in my courtroom, you cannot delegate the job of father, so don't even try. By God's grace, let's forget the fear of possible failure and start to show loving leadership in our homes. I can guarantee one thing: We *may fail* if we lovingly lead our families, but if we don't make an effort to lead, we *will fail* for sure!

Having said that, it is clear that we fathers are not alone in buying our culture's lie that our ultimate meaning and purpose is best found through a satisfying career. Mothers have been enticed by the same falsehood. A growing number of married women are either delaying or avoiding childbirth altogether, for the sake of their careers. An increasing number of women with young children are simply entering or returning to the work force, relegating childcare to babysitters and day care facilities. Data supporting the trend toward the postponing of children can be seen in the fact that in 1980, the average age of an American woman giving birth to her first born was 22.7. By 2016, the average age of having her first born was 26.3.[1]

As for employment of married women in general, in 1948, only 18% of the nation's mothers with children under eighteen worked outside of the home.[2] By 2018, this value had grown to 71%![3] While not all of them worked full-time, the vast majority (78% of the total) did, and many of their children were preschoolers. In fact, in 2018, over 65% of married women with children under the age of six were employed outside of the home for at least part of the time.

"So things have changed," someone may say. "Who says this is *really* a problem?" To me it's fairly obvious to predict the emotional, spiritual, and numerical impact of absent parents and latchkey children on our nation. To begin with, can anyone doubt that the large number of working married women has greatly reduced

---

1. https://www.thebalance.com/what-is-the-average-age-to-have-a-baby-in -the-u-s-4582455

2. "One Policy for Working Moms Won't Fit All," *Wall Street Journal*, October 29, 1986.

3. Bureau of Labor Statistics, "Employment status of the population by sex, marital status, and presence and age of own children under 18, 2017–2018 annual averages."

the population of children in our country? One of the impacts of two wage earners in families has been lowering the average size of families in America. In the 1960s, over 40 percent of Americans favored having four or more children, compared to 30 percent feeling three children were optimum, and only 18 percent wanting two children, However, by 2013, 48 percent preferred two children, 25 percent wanted three, and those desiring four or more shrank to 13 percent.[4]

Beyond the impact on population, there are other consequences as well. Even secular writers describe the emotional pain women experience when forced to choose between family and career. While much of society views a woman who selects the role of mother and full-time homemaker as an empty-headed loser, the woman who leaves her children in the care of others or who abdicates the bearing of children altogether for the sake of a career feels she is missing something. *Forbes* magazine recently published an article describing the challenge to working women with young children. The article quotes millennial mother and author E. J. Dickson, "I am constantly frustrated and frazzled, and—to be honest—angry that having children and career is still such a heroic feat."[5] The issue of mothers working outside the home is not a new one. In 1986, *Newsweek* ran a cover story on the issue "A Mother's Choice," highlighting the difficulty of pursuing both career and family. As one mother put it, "I feel guilty when I'm staying home and my associates are working, [and] I feel guilty when I'm working and my child is in someone else's care."[6]

A companion article in the same issue of *Newsweek*, "Feminism's Identity Crisis," details the dilemma of how many women have gotten much of what they have sought in terms of admission to the previously male-only corporate boardrooms, but how they are

4. George Gao, "Americans' ideal family size is smaller than it used to be." Pew Research Center, May 8, 2015; http://pewrsr.ch/1RjXPC4

5. Mary Beth Ferrante, "The Pressure is Real for Working Mothers," *Forbes*, August 27, 2018.

6. "A Mother's Choice," *Newsweek*, March 31, 1986, 48.

still feeling unfulfilled as women: "Professionals who wholeheart-edly devoted themselves to their careers speak wistfully about the children they are now too old to have."[7]

My heart goes out to thirty-nine-year-old Sharon Cohen, a childless shoe company vice-president, who publicly confessed, "My job is exciting and gratifying, but I'm haunted by the fear that I'm missing out on the most meaningful part of life by not having children.... Sometimes I imagine that if I died now my tombstone would read: 'Here lies Sharon Cohen. She read a lot of magazines.'"[8]

Ms. Cohen's refreshing honesty probably rings a responsive chord in the hearts of many thoughtful women in our country who have been led to believe that laying up treasures on earth in the form of money and career will somehow bring the deep level of life we all seek. If only it were true.

Only a few Christian couples will actually go to the extreme of being "child-free" for the sake of their career goals, but a grow-ing number will do their utmost to squeeze their child-bearing and child-rearing activities into the plan dictated by their career goals. Clearly, their jobs are their priority; children must flex to fit the pat-tern. While this approach may provide the temporary illusion that the family can have the best of both worlds, it is still a poor com-promise for both children and parents. It should be obvious without even looking at statistical data that young children need a stable, dependable, and constant parent figure to develop a good sense of who they are. Despite the irrefutable logic of this, the popular media seems to be always trying to reassure us that kids can do just fine when raised in day care centers. I'm personally more impressed with the careful work of Professor Jay Belsky, formerly of Penn State and now at the Birkbeck University of London, who, before examining the pertinent data, was of the opinion that day care for children had no negative effects. However, upon a more thorough examination

---

7. "Feminism's Identity Crisis," *Newsweek*, March 31, 1986, 58.
8. "Identity Crisis," *Newsweek*, 59.

of the many studies on the topic, Professor Belsky has radically changed his outlook. This is what he now believes to be true:

> Placing children in an average non-maternal care facility for long hours does seem to be associated with some (modest) developmental risk, especially with respect to the mother-child relationship (through first grade for Caucasian children), problem behavior (through first grade), social competence and academic work habits (by third grade) and, in adolescence, impulsivity and risk taking; and such adverse outcomes are not merely by-products of low quality child care.[9]

Apart from the emotional consequences to children who are raised in day care, there are many other problems of day care, not the least of which are the increased risk of disease and molestation. A day care licensing worker in our local community confided in me a few years ago that she was spending an inordinate amount of time responding to allegations of sexual abuse in the homes she was overseeing. Young children are so very vulnerable to abuse, and our society unfortunately has too many perverted people who seek access to children to molest them. What easier method is there to accomplish this than to establish a day care program? If you knew what I know, as a former Juvenile Court judge, about the epidemic of child sexual abuse, you would think long and hard before leaving your precious, defenseless children in the care of others, no matter how good they may look on the outside. While most day care providers will not themselves be sexually abusive, employees and teenage relatives of the providers can become perpetrators of sexual abuse in various child-care facilities and homes. Be especially alert to teen boys who seem inordinately interested in "helping" take care of young children. Parents, in your eagerness to find care for your children, be very alert and careful!

Beyond the growing risk of sexual abuse is the fact that larger day care centers, bursting at the seams with diapered children,

---

9. Jay Belsky, "Child Care and Its Impact on Young Children," Birkbeck University of London, February 2011, 2nd rev. ed., PDF version.

all naturally inclined to put objects in their mouths, and being otherwise smelly and drooling, are ideal places for the spread of infectious disease. For example, it is estimated that 15% of all infectious hepatitis cases in the U.S. are acquired through a day care facility.[10] Similarly, severe forms of diarrhea are easily spread via the "ecosystem" of the day care center. Of particular concern is the fact that the day-cared-for children have a 12.3 times higher probability of contracting the deadly disease of bacterial meningitis than home-cared-for children.[11] Obviously, the more children in a day care facility and the longer the hours of operation, the higher the likelihood of problems from disease.

For the sake of argument, let's assume a particular Christian mother has a super babysitter and her young children don't even seem to miss her when she works fifty hours or more a week. Even assuming these rather implausible facts, let me suggest three reasons why it would still not be helpful for her to pursue a career while having the responsibility of caring for young children:

1. It takes considerable income for the wife to break even economically, taking into consideration the growing cost of child care, her expanded wardrobe, transportation, and extra food expense for already prepared foods and more eating out, etc.

2. Most married women will probably bear fewer children pursuing a career than if they were full-time homemakers and mothers. If a Christian woman could just see and hug (even for a short time) the precious children God would otherwise produce through her for His glory and eternal kingdom, she would have second thoughts about pursuing

---

10. Thomas E. Ricks, "Researchers Say Day-Care Centers are Implicated in Spread of Disease," *Wall Street Journal*, September 5, 1984.

11. *Family Policy* (A Publication of the Family Research Council), May/June, 1989, quoting a study by Stephen R. Redmond, MD and Michael E. Pichichhero, MD, "Hemophilus influenzae Type b disease: An Epidemiological Study With Special Reference to Day Care Centers," *Journal of the American Medical Association*, 252, no. 18 (November 9, 1984).

a full-time career and motherhood simultaneously. Intrinsically, we all know this is the truth.

3. This woman is forfeiting one of the most important roles as a mother: to influence the next generation in godly ways. Mary Pride, author of *The Way Home*, was a radical feminist activist prior to her conversion to Christ in 1977.[12] Mary's book approaches the issue of women and careers from her unique perspective as a former feminist. One of her primary themes is to encourage Christian women to obey the scriptural injunction to "love their husbands...[and] children, to be discreet, chaste, homemakers, good, obedient to their own husbands, that the word of God may not be blasphemed" (Titus 2:4–5).

Mary summarizes the choice for women: "For us young wives, it boils down to this: *are we willing to obey God*, to love our husbands and children, to be self-controlled and pure, to work *at home* (not the office), to be kind, and to be subject to our husbands, so that no one will blaspheme the Word of God? Are we out to nurture our families, putting others first, or to destroy our churches and country, putting ourselves first? Will we rock the cradle, or cradle the rock?"[13] Mary does a marvelous job in her book of suggesting ways for women to cope with the demands of life at home full of positive activities for God that are eternally and infinitely more fulfilling than a career could ever be.

Let me return to talking to both fathers and mothers. Often it's we husbands who literally shove our wives out the door to work because *we* want more of this world's goods. As you recall from the first part of this book, I essentially did this myself for the first two years of our marriage. My wife, Marcia, became a very successful teacher. But God was working in her heart, and she wanted a child much more than she wanted to continue working. And to her credit, Marcia has never wanted to return to work outside of the home.

---

12. Mary Pride, *The Way Home* (Westchester, Ill.: Crossway Books, 1985).
13. Pride, *Way Home*, 208.

However, if we had only a couple of children, I'm sure her attitude may have changed (she doesn't like to be bored). It's quite possible that many intelligent women resort to careers because of the lack of meaningful and challenging work in the home due to small numbers of children. The desire for careers and small family sizes go hand in hand.

The bottom line is this: in just a few brief years, each of us will be making the trip to eternity. How much of our bank accounts or careers or fancy clothes, expensive cars, or other toys will we be able to take to heaven with us? Obviously, the answer is none of these things. But we *can* take our children with us if we trust our covenant-keeping God to bring them there, using us in the process by His amazing grace, through the powerful, converting Holy Spirit who is pleased to bless the spiritual disciplines we use in rearing them. Jesus said, "of such is the kingdom of heaven" (Matt. 19:14). May our heavenly Father help us to see the truth of this today.

CHAPTER 12

The Physical Argument

**"Bearing and raising more children will
cause me numerous physical problems."**

Picture in your mind's eye "Old Mother Hubbard," who had so many children she didn't know what to do with them all. If you are like me, I can clearly visualize this frazzled forty-five-year-old woman, looking like she's sixty, wearing a dirty apron, her mouth agape, and a distant, helpless gaze in her tired, twitching eyes. But Old Mother Hubbard was fictitious. What do mothers of large families actually look like?

In my many travels, I've seen lots of mothers with large families. Recently, I met a couple in Massachusetts with fifteen children. I honestly couldn't believe how slender and young they *both* looked. Almost without exception, mothers of very large families (eight or more children) look lovely, mature, satisfied, and feminine. My wife, Marcia, now in her early 70s, is "Exhibit A" of this tendency, but I have seen many other women who look similarly young and radiant (but none as beautiful as Marcia!).

God created women to give birth and to expand the human race. Certainly pregnancy can take its toll on stomach muscles and leg circulation in some women. My wife's legs are somewhat discolored from bearing twelve children, but her weight dropped back to about 120 pounds between pregnancies (with God's help, she would have me add), and her general health is excellent. And we both agree that our very special children created in God's image and destined to live with Him forever are totally worth the temporary inconvenience of a few visible leg veins. Children generally keep their parents thinking, acting, and feeling young. Our children need us as parents, and this need seems to prompt our bodies and souls to rise to meet the challenge. Frankly, we are too busy to grow old early!

On a related issue is the fear perpetrated everywhere of the dangers associated with becoming pregnant after age thirty-five or forty. As Mary Pride explains in her book:

> I am willing to grant that a woman who has her first child past age forty is likely to have problems, as is one who has been using birth control for years and slips up at that late date. You would *expect* a female body that had been lying barren for so many years, in which all the healthiest young eggs had already been lost, to have trouble adjusting to pregnancy. And then there are the cumulative effects of years of chemical dosage. Coming off the pill, a woman's hormones may not yet have gotten the message that they are supposed to function normally now.[1]

The American College of Obstetrics and Gynecology and the federal government's National Institute of Child Health are in agreement that "with minor qualifications, a healthy 35-year-old, or older, can look forward to as safe a pregnancy and as healthy an infant as a woman in her early 20s."[2] They conceded in their articles that this conclusion flies in the face of prevailing widely held beliefs. This conclusion was based on factual studies performed in various places in the United States, and has garnered the support of the medical organizations previously listed.

The data shows that while older women miscarry more often, they actually are less prone to suffer from maternal fever and are more likely to deliver a baby of normal birth weight than younger mothers. The older pregnant woman is somewhat more likely than

---

1. Pride, *Way Home*, 51.
2. "Pregnancy Past 35 No Longer Seen Such A Risk," *Grand Rapids Press*, April 2, 1986.

her younger counterpart to have adult-onset diabetes and high blood pressure, but these conditions can usually be controlled through careful prenatal care. The study concluded: "When they are given good prenatal and intrapartum care, and when the signs of hypertension and diabetes are monitored, the risks to healthy women 35 years and older...may be no more than the risks of the younger [women]."[3]

Mary Pride, in her typically direct manner, turns the question on its head: "What about," she asks, "the medical dangers of *not* having children?" Apparently there is some thought that breast and cervical cancer may well be due to the lack of pregnancies in our culture and the consequent stress on the reproductive system caused by women who ovulate so frequently in their adult lives.[4]

Mary Pride and feminist Germaine Greer (from opposite sides) join forces in decrying the use of the pill and the IUD as truly being contrary to the medical best interests of women. Taken orally, the birth control pill contains hormones that touch all the parts of the body, yet are really targeted for only the reproductive system. These hormones are consumed daily, month after month, by women all over the globe. I find it moving that feminist, pro-abortionist Germaine Greer speaks so passionately against the pill in *Sex and Destiny*; her research on the subject appears impeccable.[5] Since her publication of this book, even more evidence has come to light linking the pill to breast cancer in younger women.

In recent years, the big push has been to get "back to basics" by removing artificial ingredients from our food, exercising more, breathing fresh air, drinking pure water, etc. Isn't it amazing that amid their rigorous health food diets and expensive exercise clubs, otherwise intelligent women voluntarily ingest potent sex steroids every day, chemically telling their bodies they are pregnant, thus

---

3. "Pregnancy Past 35," *Grand Rapids Press*.

4. Pride, *Way Home*, 52.

5. Germaine Greer, *Sex and Destiny* (New York: Harper and Row, 1984), 163ff.

rendering them temporarily sterile, or even aborting any newly formed conceptus?

Women over the centuries have been conceiving and bearing children for many thousands of years longer than they have been consuming these birth control pills. Isn't it much more "back to nature" and healthier, all things being equal, to bear children, than to practice the new ways that oppose nature? Shouldn't we trust God to get us through childbirth and not give us more challenges than we can handle? Who owns us anyhow?

CHAPTER 13

The Unfashionable Argument

**"It is not popular to have more than two
or three children; I don't want to be
unfashionable by having a large family."**

Not too many years ago, large families were viewed as signs of God's blessing; now society often looks down its nose at couples who have more than two or three children. Most cultures and groups do shun individuals who depart significantly from what is considered normal. And it is certainly considered abnormal today to have a large family. Hence, if being fashionable is important to you, you will have only two, or at the most three, children. Taking modern day fashion in this area to the extreme are those generally upscale couples who voluntarily choose to have no children at all as they chase dollars, or careers, or whatever else they feel is more important.

One of many books on this subject, *Marriage Without Children*, documents the practice of intentional childlessness in detail.[1] The author, Diana Burgwyn, says that pro-childbirth feelings abounded in this country until the peak year of the baby boom, in 1957. "And then something happened to change it all. Or, rather, several things."[2] The factors Burgwyn considers significant include: the feminist movement with its philosophy of choice in reproductive

---

1. Diana Burgwyn, *Marriage Without Children* (New York: Harper and Row, 1981).

2. Burgwyn, *Marriage*, 6.

matters and the growing realization that raising a child is often a thankless duty in modern society. Adding to this were the high rate of divorce, later marriages, freer sex both in and out of marriage, more dependable birth control, and legalized abortion.[3]

But, according to Burgwyn, the one issue that really gave social legitimacy to intentional childlessness was the "overpopulation" issue of the late 1960s. Says Burgwyn: "To say you are doing something for the good of humanity [like being sterilized for population concerns] sounds much better than to admit that you just don't want children."[4]

To help couples in their decision to be "childfree" (which was apparently viewed as liberating as being germ-free, trouble-free, and carefree), support groups were established around the country. One such group, the National Organization for Non-Parents (NON), was formed in 1972. Perhaps feeling their name was a bit harsh for popular consumption, NON became the National Alliance for Optional Parenthood (NAOP) in 1978. Members included Hugh Downs, John Simon, Shirley MacLaine, Paul Ehrlich, and Lee Salk. On the first of August of each year, NAOP held an annual "Non-Parents' Day." Their first bash in 1974 included three women in white, dancing a "non-fertility rite." The highlight of each year's gathering was to see which outstanding man and woman would be named the non-father and non-mother of the year.[5] Burgwyn, who was obviously sympathetic with society's growing acceptance of optional parenthood, reserved her greatest condemnation for what she called the "most tenacious pro-natalist holdout" in our culture. What is this great enemy of the childfree lifestyle? "Religions," she said. Maybe in 1981, when the book was written, religions were still advocating for children and childbirth, but I think it is fair to say that it is certainly not the case now. The perspective that children

---

3. Burgwyn, *Marriage*, 6.
4. Burgwyn, *Marriage*, 11.
5. Burgwyn, *Marriage*, 15.

are, at most, a qualified blessing has garnered nearly universal support in our culture.

Germaine Greer devotes the bulk of her *Sex and Destiny* to develop her major thesis that,

> the modern Western infant is wanted by fewer people than any infants in our long history, not only by fewer parents, but by smaller groups of people.... Historically, human societies have been pro-child; modern society is unique in that it is profoundly hostile to children. We in the West do not refrain from childbirth because we are concerned about the population explosion or because we feel we cannot afford children, but because we do not like children.[6]

Greer, while being neither Christian nor pro-life, nonetheless does an excellent job of contrasting our culture's contempt for children with the attitude people in less developed countries have toward children: "My association with Italian peasants and with South Indian women and aborigines offered endless examples of the undemanding pleasure which children give to non-materialistic peoples, for whom they are the only entertainment and the reason for undergoing all the hardships which are their daily life."[7]

Newsweek magazine did a cover story on the issue of married couples who have chosen to be childless. Featured in the article were a number of double income couples literally gushing with enthusiasm about the joys and freedoms of the childfree life. To me, the most tragic quote was from one of the intentionally childless women, Diana Card Linden, who had recently had a scare with an "almost child":

> For Diana Card Linden, 40, a neurobiologist in Los Angeles, the time of reckoning came last year, when she found out she was pregnant. It was accidental; although she has always loved children, she never felt they belonged in her life. Her husband (Charles), a 37 year-old dermatologist, doesn't like kids, but

---

6. Greer, *Sex and Destiny*, 2.
7. Greer, *Sex and Destiny*, 260.

she had always believed that if she wanted a baby, he would go along with it. With the pregnancy, there was suddenly a choice to confront. "I considered the way I wanted my life to be," she says. "I decided I would have to make a lot of changes that I was not willing to make if I was going to have a child." She and her husband discussed what to do and finally decided that Diana should have an abortion. "I knew it was the right thing for me to do, but that doesn't stop me thinking about it or questioning what I did," she says. "As a biologist, I know that when I had the abortion, I killed something living. I have no rationalization, no explanation for that. And that bothers me. It also bothers me because I was 39 and that's sort of a do-or-die age if you're going to have a child."[8]

Isn't this incredibly sad? Can't you imagine these people, twenty or thirty years from now, facing old age alone? And they are in the medical field. Of all people, they will always really know—especially in their eventual loneliness—that they killed their only child. Whenever we put God and His ways out of our lives, we turn life on its head and cause great problems for ourselves and our world.

Truly, apart from a godly willingness to live unselfishly, having children makes little sense in the short run. The immediate payback in raising a child is minuscule in comparison to the amount of work required day in and day out to do it right. You have to wait a long time; indeed, your real reward for raising a child may not even come in this lifetime. It is hard to be self-centered and a successful parent at the same time. But because our culture condones living for self and still believes in the myth of overpopulation, couples who intentionally spend their time and money on themselves—without children—are often respected more than other couples who sacrifice and raise large families. I'm still waiting for Newsweek to do an equally upbeat cover story on large families!

---

8. "Three's a Crowd," *Newsweek*, 74.

How can we respond to this objection? First, we seldom, if ever, find lasting happiness by going along with the crowd. Even in a purely human sense, we need to learn to be true to ourselves rather than catering to some arbitrary societal expectation. And most people—sooner or later—begin to feel the dawning of a God-given longing to raise children, despite the costs and occasional headaches involved.

People's innate desire for children is documented, perhaps to show the vestiges of the "old way of thinking," by Diana Burgwyn, in her book, *Marriage Without Children*. She quotes Dr. Sherman J. Silker, urologist and microsurgeon at a medical center in St. Louis, who is an expert in performing vasectomy reversals. Based on his experience, Dr. Silker feels it is unwise for childless men to be sterilized at all: "I have met so many men who said they never wanted children at all—twenty-one, twenty-five-year-old men who were absolutely against the concept of children—and then five or ten years later, for reasons I don't understand (and they can't articulate it very well either), they come back wanting to have children."[9]

Women often have similar feelings. Burgwyn interviewed a thirty-four-year-old woman named Rachel about her changing views:

> Our attitude about what is of value in life has changed over time. We've been married twelve years. We've done our traveling and other things that we wanted to do, and as time passed, we found ourselves asking, "What is the purpose of life on this planet? Why are we here? How can we best make a contribution?" I've given teaching [she was a high school math teacher] my best shot, and while I'm not eager to bail out of it for psychological, as well as financial reasons, it's not enough. We both realize that these are very hard times—a hard culture to raise a child in—and neither of us is a risk-taker. But not to take a risk is to remain on the career path, which I think for me is a somewhat sterile [no pun intended, I'm sure], dead-end path. What appears to be a very comfortable nook can become an upholstered cell. And one thing I have seen among a lot of

---

9. Burgwyn, *Marriage*, 88.

voluntarily childless couples which I do not like is an emphasis on hedonism, whether it is material possessions, careers, pets, travel, or even causes.[10]

Life is much more than maximizing the fun and minimizing the pain in the short run. A life based on true wisdom is concerned primarily with long-range implications. While we have been focusing on couples that carry anti-child attitudes to the extreme, the same arguments may apply for couples who, for the sake of being fashionable or self-centered, stop at the "millionaire's family" size of two—the boy and the girl, or stop at three children. The question to all of us remains the same: Who are we living for: ourselves or God? Are we willing to be unfashionable for God's sake, or are we too worried about what others will say? Remember the proverb: "The fear of man brings a snare, but whoever trusts in the Lord shall be safe" (Prov. 29:25). God sees the end from the beginning. He often allows His children to be buffeted by trials and problems in the short run to experience long-term gain.

Children are certainly a short-term trial. Mind you, they do bring joy quite often, but the joy is almost always mixed with some work or concern on our part. Yet in the final analysis, we know that we shall ultimately "reap a harvest if we do not give up." We expect teenagers who are acutely aware of peer pressure to be worried about whether or not their conduct matches the norm. What parent of a teen has not heard "I am the only one who has to do this (or can't do that"? While we expect this from teenagers, God expects more from us. He rightly expects us to resist the temptation to go with the flow of society when it opposes His perspectives. And if enough of us obey God in this area, we will change our culture!

---

10. Burgwyn, *Marriage*, 139.

CHAPTER 14

The Selfish Argument

**"I don't want to have the number of children
that I definitely would have if we
did not practice 'family planning.'"**

After all, who wants ten kids? Actually, there are a lot worse scourges that could happen to a Christian couple than to have ten or more children. Last I checked, Psalm 127 is still in the Bible and assures us that children are indeed a blessing, like arrows in one's quiver. In the "good ol' days," it was relatively common for families to have ten or more children. Certainly since the *average* American woman in the year 1800 had seven children, there must have been some very large families to balance out those women who remained single or otherwise could bear no children.

So while large families are exceedingly rare today, they flourished in prior generations, when many women had many children with few or no ill effects, emotionally or physically. Therefore, if God should grant you the fantastic privilege of raising ten children, each of whom is created in His image and who possesses the potential of living forever in His eternal kingdom, such a "predicament" would be far from the torturous experience suggested by modern society today.

But there is solid reason to believe—both biblically and medically—that the vast majority of couples who decide to let God be sovereign in their reproductive lives, will not have inordinately large families. We all know of couples who would literally give anything if they could conceive and bear even *one* child. How I grieve for these dear people! But we must ultimately conclude that our Father knows best. Scripture contains many instances of God closing the womb and opening the womb (Gen. 29:31, 35; 30:2, 9, 17, 22; Judg. 13:3; 1 Sam. 1:5, 19, 20; 1 Sam. 2:21). Certainly we cannot conclude that conceiving a child is anything other than the work of God Himself. I am not suggesting, however, that it is medically wrong to treat a diagnosed problem of infertility. But we must always view the "making" of children as God's work, not merely a result of chance, plus time and biological material.

We can get some idea of how many children to expect by looking at the genealogies of the Old Testament. First Chronicles, for example, documents the number of children certain people had when children were viewed as an unmitigated blessing. While some fathers listed in 1 Chronicles had twelve and thirteen children (1 Chron. 1:20-23; 29-31), others had one (1 Chron. 2:8, 36) or none at all (1 Chron. 2:30, 32). Listen to a statement made in the midst of the genealogies: "Shimei [of the tribe of Simeon] had sixteen sons and six daughters; but his brothers did not have many children, nor did any of their families multiply as much as the children of Judah" (1 Chron. 4:27).

Another rather moving account concerns Obed-Edom and his family. Obed-Edom was the fortunate man who happened to live on the road where the ark of the covenant was being transported en route to the temple from the land of the Philistines where it had earlier been taken captive. Problems developed during the trip and the ark had to be placed in temporary quarters. Obed-Edom's home was selected. There would have been ample reasons for Obed-Edom *not* to want the ark in his home. For one, it brought severe sickness to many of the Philistines and resulted in the untimely death of an Israelite man who instinctively tried to steady the ark during transport, but in a way contrary to the law of God. This ark was very powerful! But Obed-Edom trusted in the goodness of God and welcomed the ark into his home for three months. The result: "The Lord blessed the house of Obed-Edom and all that he had"

(1 Chron. 13:14). How did God bless Obed-Edom? The author of 1 Chronicles lists Obed-Edom's eight sons by name and then adds the phrase, "for God blessed him" (1 Chron. 26:5). He had been blessed with children!

Mary Pride quotes data suggesting that the average woman would have only five or six children in her lifetime if contraceptives were universally eliminated.[1] These numbers are certainly consistent with the average of seven children per woman in the U.S. in 1800, prior to family planning being employed. Mary Pride describes her own experience of not being able to conceive a child until she and her husband specifically *prayed* for another child. She had borne only four children at the time she wrote her book *The Way Home*. While this is obviously not everyone's experience, God *is* divinely involved in the conception of every child.

My wife, Marcia, has also found it necessary to pray before being able to conceive any of our twelve children. Having this many children is not particularly easy, but neither is it that difficult. It isn't particularly easy to raise one or two children either. Every parent I've ever met is already largely overwhelmed with the responsibility, regardless of the number. But we can rest in the assurance that God always gives us the ability to do what He calls us to do: "God's call is God's enablement."

The conclusion: Your chances of having a dozen or more children is remote, even without contraception. But we undoubtedly will have more children without contraception and sterilization than with these practices. How many will be up to the God who loves us and knows what we really can handle financially, emotionally, and otherwise. We keep coming back to this basic point: Can we *really* trust God, and will we obey Him in this critical area?

---

1. Pride, *Way Home*, 64–79.

CHAPTER 15

The Heartache Argument

**"This world is such a dangerous place:
I want to cut the odds of heartache and
pain by having few or no children."**

Many couples choose not to have more children because they are afraid of the future. For some parents this fear is significant, while for others, it is negligible.

Truly, life today is dangerous for children: we hear and read almost daily of children being assaulted, molested, and murdered. We live under the constant threat of terrorist bombings, crippling disease, and accidents, not to mention the daily temptations of drugs, alcohol, immorality, and other hazardous allurements. How can we ensure that our children will be protected from these dangers? Aren't we better off with fewer children to safeguard?

In response, aren't we Christians supposed to live for God, not for self-protection? Bear in mind that it is just as sinful to *fail* to do what God wants us to do as it is sinful to do what we shouldn't do.

As I look within my own heart, I find more cowardice than I'd like to admit. By nature, we tend to move away from risks and toward comfort and safety. We work feverishly to organize our lives, assets, and plans and feel we don't really need God to help us on a daily basis. We find it easier to trust our government, homes, security systems, bank accounts, attorneys, automobiles, insurance, etc., than to trust in an invisible, yet all-powerful and loving God. How far we have strayed from the attitude that David had:

Truly my soul silently waits for God;
From Him comes my salvation.
He only is my rock and my salvation;
He is my defense; I shall not be greatly moved. (Ps. 62:1–2)

Children make us much more vulnerable, much more depen-
dent upon God. This makes us very uncomfortable. We long for
more control over our own happiness. But, let's face it: we are not
in absolute control of our own lives. It is only by God's minute-by-
minute sustaining hand that our hearts and minds keep working.
People who attempt to create their version of heaven on earth are
called fools by God. In Luke 12:18–21, we read of one such rich
fool. Listen to his egocentric comments:

> So he said, "*I* will do this: *I* will pull down *my* barns and build
> greater, and there *I* will store all *my* crops and *my* goods. And
> *I'll* say to *my* soul, 'Soul, you have many goods laid up for
> many years; take your ease; eat, drink, and be merry.'" (Luke
> 12:18–21) (emphasis added)

What did God do to this proud man? He ended the man's life
that very night. The rich man's property was given to another. Jesus's
closing editorial comment was, "So is he who lays up treasure for
himself, and is not rich toward God." We need to be rich toward
God, which always bears the fruit of obeying God courageously
and selflessly. That includes submitting ourselves to God in the
important area of child-bearing and child-raising. Once we choose
to embrace God's will in our lives, despite the cost, we can draw
comfort and peace from promises in God's Word for the protection
for our families. For example:

> This poor man cried out, and the LORD heard him,
> And saved him out of all his troubles.
> The angel of the Lord encamps all around those who fear Him,
> And delivers them. (Ps. 34:6–7)

We see in Scripture how David and his growing family were
marvelously delivered from danger, time and time again, as they
trusted and obeyed God. David lived in very threatening times

and circumstances. He was constantly pursued by King Saul's best soldiers. But, to quote the old cliché, "God plus one makes a majority." One day David returned with his fighting men to the town of Ziklag in the land of Gath. Upon their arrival, David and his men were horrified with what they saw: the city was burned, and all their wives, children, and possessions had been taken by the raiding Amalekites. Clearly, bad things can happen to good people. The response of David and his men was most understandable: "Then David and the people who were with him lifted up their voices and wept, until they had no more power to weep" (1 Sam. 30:4). David's men even talked of killing David, since "each man was grieved, every man for his sons and his daughters" (v. 6). These men were *hurting*. Their wives and their children had been kidnapped. These macho warriors cried shamelessly and uncontrollably.

I love the next sentence of Scripture. This verse should encourage us the next time we are down or doubting: "But David strengthened himself in the LORD his God" (v. 6). The passage doesn't say how David turned from grief to trust; perhaps he reflected on God's protection in the past and meditated on the Word of God. He may have recounted the story of the children of Israel at the Red Sea, who, with the Egyptians at their backs, saw their deliverance when God parted the waters. In any event, God met David at this low point. And how we need to do the same!

David prayed for guidance, and then, led by God, began a swift campaign to reclaim the wives, children, and possessions. Soon their despair changed to rejoicing. "And nothing of theirs was lacking, either small or great, sons or daughters, spoil or anything which they had taken from them" (v. 19). Not only did they recover their own goods, but David and his men also became owners of the plunder the Amalekites had taken from other Philistine cities (v. 16). By enduring temporary pain, David and his men were compensated with a growth of faith and a growth of resources. What a marked contrast between this exciting episode of God's protection of David and his family, and a time later in David's life when his family was devastated due to his own sinful choices.

Did God forget to protect David's family at that time? No. David simply ceased being the righteous leader and protector his family needed, and thereby allowed evil forces to enter and devour his children. We all know of the major sin in David's later life: first there was his adultery with Bathsheba, the wife of Uriah the Hittite; and then the murder of Uriah to cover up Bathsheba's pregnancy.. To David's credit, when confronted with his sin, he did not follow in the ways of his predecessor King Saul by blaming others. He confessed his sin to God. And David was forgiven.

But (and, as Christians, we need to learn this), we can be judicially cleared of a sin in God's account book and yet still suffer the logical and natural consequences of our sin on earth. Forgiveness of sin does not eliminate all the consequences of sin. The alcoholic will be forgiven his sin of drinking to excess, but his liver and other organs will still show the effects of his drinking. The man or woman who cheaply sells his or her purity to gain a measure of temporal enjoyment or popularity will suffer the spiritual, emotional, and physical consequences of sin, despite being forgiven by God if asked of Him.

It is indeed ironic (though altogether just) that later in David's life, his own children mirrored David's particular sins, bringing a painful reminder of the grief, pain, guilt, and sorrow that sin brings. In 2 Samuel 13, we read how David's son Amnon raped his half-sister Tamar. If this were not bad enough, David himself summoned Tamar to come to Amnon's bedside, where the sexual assault occurred. As an alert father, David should have spiritually discerned Amnon's evil, immoral intentions in asking that Tamar come to his bedside to feed him. But David's spiritual eyes had been clouded by his own sin, which occurred many years before, and he passed the request to Tamar, to David's disgrace and shame.

Two years later, David again played the fool when he unwittingly orchestrated the circumstances which led to one of his sons murdering another. The tragedy, detailed in 2 Samuel 13:23ff., began when David, at his son Absalom's request, sent Absalom's half-brother Amnon to a family party in Baal Hazor. Absalom had secretly planned this event as an occasion to avenge the rape of his full-sister Tamar. Why didn't David spiritually suspect Absalom's devious intentions? Was he blinded by his own past sin of murder?

Similarly, as parents, we are blinded in areas of our own weakness and past failures. I regret to say that I have seen this in painful ways in my own life. Fathers and mothers, we cannot afford even a little area of sin in thought, attitude, or deed. Our families will suffer if we do. I have found my acknowledgment of this responsibility motivates me to be rigorously righteous when I am otherwise tempted to be careless. Our families' biggest enemies are often ourselves, rather than external forces. This can be both bad and good. It can be bad that we have to accept the responsibility for many of our own problems. It can be good because, with God's power, we can change and strengthen the walls of protection for our families. There is no evil so great that it can overwhelm God's ability to protect our children.

One final point in this area: There is a degree to which a large family may provide more protection from evil onslaughts than a small family does. One of the biggest and potentially most destructive influences on our children as they mature is their friends. If God provides you with a large family and you adhere to God's principles and help these unique children grow in godly character, they will spend much of their time playing with each other. And let's face it: siblings can become lifelong friends—not just short-term school buddies. In our family, it really is true that our children's best friends are their own brothers and sisters. This attitude of mutual caring and love impresses other people who see our family, and this prompts many positive comments. Oh sure, we have our share of intra-familial hassles and arguments. But we prayerfully use God's Word (see Matt. 18:15ff.) to deal with such problems and to keep the emotional air clear. It *really* is great (most of the time)!

Not too long ago an associate lost his only child, a seventeen-year-old son, who died from a congenital medical problem after exercising strenuously. The best efforts to revive the child failed. I felt deeply for this man and his wife. If I lost one of my children, I believe I would hurt as much as this man, even though I would still have eleven others. It's not like you've lost one of twelve dollars and can say: "At least I have eleven left." No, but by grace, you love each child sincerely and deeply.

But having said this, the parents of multiple children, while no doubt aching for the loss of a child, can (more effectively perhaps) go on with life after grieving. That parent continues to have a hold on the future. He or she can still experience the blessings of being a grandparent. When a crisis like this occurs there can be strength in numbers. Limiting children to what we believe we can handle is not God's way of protecting us from a frightening world. What we must do is obey God, and trust Him, knowing that He will never leave us or forsake us.

CHAPTER 16

The Inability Argument

**"I can't handle the children I have now;
I couldn't think of having any more!"**

Occasionally when I speak to groups and attempt to encourage those in the audience to be open to God for the children He would like to bless them and the world with, a frustrated woman will approach me, quite upset at the thought of having another child. She can't handle raising the children she has now, and the suggestion of having more seems impossible to her.

Without a doubt, spending a rainy afternoon in a bungalow big enough for two with a menacing cadre of hyperactive, preschool boys, possessing more jumpy energy than a beehive in the summertime, is not one's idea of a frolic in the park. And then to even *think* about adding a colicky baby to this indoor zoo seems almost certain to ensure the need to send in reinforcements. Then there is the concern about how bad it would be for this new child to grow up in a crowded home with tired, hassled, and overworked parents. Without a doubt, for some families, chaos reigns supreme most of the time. Almost all families with young children (and many with older ones) have occasional times of stress. What parent (in his or her weaker moments) does not at least *entertain* the thought of offering one of his troublesome children up for sale for a nominal price? We never *really* would do it, of course, but parenting occasionally does tempt us to want to resign, if only we could figure out where to turn in our resignation papers!

In all seriousness, however, despite the seasons of stress, the reality is that thousands upon thousands of parents over the years have not only survived the experience of raising a large group of children: most wouldn't trade it for anything. The children of many of these families, rather than feeling neglected, unloved, and resentful, speak in warm and glowing terms of their families. They still treasure their large family gatherings, where they can relive some of their great memories from the past.

How can you explain the phenomenon of happy, large families? I've heard different theories to explain them, such as, "The parents of these successful, large families are simply geniuses"; or sometimes just the opposite: "These parents are too ignorant to know any better." Or, "They just got lucky, and had children who were *perfect angels*." Based on my experience, and having seen many large families in juvenile court, and being the father of twelve children myself, I can say that there are factors far more significant than family size that influence the "joy index" of any given family. That is to say, there are both happy and unhappy small families, just as there are both happy and unhappy large families. Adding a child to a fundamentally dysfunctional family will only make matters worse, while adding a child to a growing and communicating family will only make things better.

For the Christian family with a degree of purpose, healthy communication, and shared values, another child is a cause for great joy, since, with each new child, there is a new person to share and add to the love bond of the family. It's like playing music with a full orchestra rather than a brass ensemble or a duet of two instruments. It's painting with *all* the colors of the rainbow, and not just with two or three. More children add depth, style, and harmony to the Christian family. But just as more children can enhance the welfare of a solid family, they can also aggravate the problems of a dysfunctional family. More children will seldom, if ever, turn chaos into order, or grief into joy. Regardless of the health of a family, it is true that raising one or more little boys can be a very difficult, thankless, and seemingly endless endeavor. Little girls are not always easy either!

But the comforting truth is that things *will* get easier relatively quickly. One of the most difficult times of parenting that my wife and I can recall was when we had three little girls. When you have two, each adult can take care of one child; but with three children, it becomes more challenging. Things actually get easier when your oldest children start to mature, and begin to lend their own hands, feet, brains, and hearts to help with the younger children. Unless you take unfair advantage of this, older siblings will not usually resent playing with or helping younger kids. They enjoy assisting the baby (most of the time) and are invaluable as playmates—providing another set of eyes and ears to be alert to danger.

When Marcia and I had our first child, Michelle, I didn't think it would be possible to love another child as much as I loved our first-born. So I was surprised to see that God supplied the same quantity of love for our second-born, Renee, and for each of our subsequent children as they arrived. And this love flows, not only through the parents, but through the other children as well. Our last three children were literally inundated with love from us as well as from their older brothers and sisters who often fought for the right to hold their little brothers or sister.

Without the essential building blocks necessary for raising a joyful family, including the active involvement of *both* parents—along with discipline, mutual respect, communication, and structure—a family will not experience much success, regardless of its size. But when a family follows godly principles, its "joy quotient" cannot help but grow, and the more children around to share in this joy, the merrier.

CHAPTER 17

The Medical Argument

"God obviously favors contraception since He has
sovereignly allowed medical science to create it."

***

Part 1: The Beginnings of the Movement to Limit Children
There is both a short and a long response to this statement. The
short response is simply that if everything medical science discovers
is automatically consistent with God's revealed will, then we are all
in a lot of trouble. Medical "science" has developed abortion, various forms of euthanasia, and even the "harvesting" of fetal tissue for
research, none of which can be supported scripturally.

It's illogical to suggest that while God holds man responsible for
his own sins in general, any actions by man performed under the title
of "science" are somehow beyond the pale of God's scrutiny. Isn't it
possible for man to sin by manipulating nature? Hitler's technicians,
who performed hideous experiments on the handicapped, Jewish
people, and other "undesirables," are proof enough that "science,"
when practiced by sinful men, can be a tool of incredible evil. While
it may be scientifically feasible to control an entire nation by placing
certain drugs in the drinking water, the vast majority of Christians
would agree that such a plan is morally and spiritually wrong. Science only tells us what is possible; it does not tell us what is right.

There is a longer answer to the statement of this chapter. And
that answer involves a closer look at the history of the movement
to limit births in the Western world. The results of such an analysis reveal much about the motives and actions of those who have

been advancing contraception during the last two centuries. In the remainder of this chapter, and in the following chapter, we will consider a much-abbreviated history of the efforts to restrict children through contraception and other means. We will see that the movement to separate sex from the possibility of reproduction has been as much a philosophical and religious movement as it has been a medical issue.

I daresay that most people are of the opinion that birth control is of relatively recent vintage, starting with the invention of "the pill" in the 1950s, and continuing with the birth control pill's widespread acceptance by the public in the 1960s. However, those who are more informed about this issue will remind us of the groundbreaking "family planning" work in the early 1900s, by such notable birth control pioneers as Margaret Sanger, who founded Planned Parenthood.

While this is closer to the actual beginnings of birth control in Western nations, a more accurate statement would be that the intentional prevention of conception has existed in one form or another for thousands of years. In fact, with only few exceptions, almost all human cultures have practiced some form of child limitation. Birth control historian Norman E. Himes puts it this way: "Man's attempts to control the increase of his numbers reach so far back into the dim past that it is impossible to discern their real origin. Some forms of limitation on the rate of increase are undoubtedly as old as the life history of man."[1]

The methods used by various cultures to limit children has, of course, greatly varied, but the results have largely been the same: the number of people in a given family, tribe, or nation are lower than they otherwise would be.

The primary means used to accomplish birth limitation over the centuries have included prolonged abstention from sexual

---

1. Norman E. Himes, *Medical History of Contraception* (1936; repr., New York: Gamut Press, 1963), 3.

intercourse between married people, abortion, and infanticide.[2] The method of performing infanticide often involved customs such as: (1) killing every other child born, (2) killing every child born after the third, and (3) killing any child born too close to the preceding child.[3]

According to population expert A. M. Carr-Saunders, both abortion and infanticide have been widely practiced "in Asiatic countries up to within living memory, and in Europe up to the beginning of the Christian era."[4]

Himes likewise supports the view that abortion and infanticide have historically been the most commonly used methods of limiting births in primitive societies. But the primary focus of Himes's classic work concerns the medical history of contraception, and the practices engaged in over the years to prevent conception altogether.[5] He concludes that most of the primitive attempts at contraception were based on "old wives' tales" or superstitious magic, rather than on scientific principles, and therefore were not really effective in preventing pregnancy.

However, due to what Himes feels has been mankind's lengthy fascination with family limitation, he simply concludes that it (anti-conception) must fulfill "some fundamental human need. It has shown great sticking power. It has not only survived; it has grown increasingly strong."[6]

Assuming, for sake of argument, the truth of Himes's last statement, we must conclude that Western Judeo-Christian society is tragically deprived compared to primitive societies in having this "fundamental human need" met, since, as we shall see, contraception, abortion, and infanticide have traditionally been considered immoral by both Jews and Christians. Carr-Saunders touches on

---

2. A. M. Carr-Saunders, *Population* (London: Oxford University Press, 1925), 15.

3. Carr-Saunders, *Population*, 15-16.

4. Carr-Saunders, *Population*, 18-19.

5. Himes, *Medical History*, 4.

6. Himes, *Medical History*, xxxvi.

this contrast: "The Christian era witnessed a profound change. Abortion and infanticide were rendered illegal."[7]

If this assertion is true, did the populations in Judeo-Christian nations burgeon out of control? No. And Carr-Saunders helps explain why. Apparently, without abortion and infanticide available in Europe during the Middle Ages, it became customary for couples to delay marriage and more widely practice celibacy "for the first time in the history of the world."[8] The immediate cause of this marital delay and celibacy was the feudal system, with its compulsory apprentice program. Until sufficient money was saved, or apprenticeships completed, marriage was virtually out of the question. Hence, fewer children were born. Other factors that restricted population growth, according to Carr-Saunders, included the growth of cities and the consequent spread of plagues and other epidemics, as well as frequent battles and wars.

How about the use of contraception in "Christian" nations to restrict births? Peter Fryer, in his detailed history of the birth control movement, researched medieval references to the subject. Hampering him in his study, however, was an obstacle: "Partly because of religious prejudices, and partly because of ignorance, the concept of limiting births [through contraception] was closely linked during this period with two other detested practices: abortion and anal coitus. So it is hard to dissociate contraceptive practices from abortion; the language used in medieval texts could often refer to either or both."[9]

Even in the 1400's, some form of contraception was being practiced (though most certainly not with moral approval) as is evident by a piece from Chaucer in *The Parson's Tale*:

> Eek whan man destourbeth concepcioun of a child, and maketh a womman outher bareyne by drynkyge venenouse herbes thurgh which she may not conceyve, or sleeth a child

---

7. Carr-Saunders, *Population*, 19.
8. Carr-Saunders, *Population*, 19.
9. Peter Fryer, *The Birth Controllers* (New York: Stein and Day, 1966), 21.

by drynkes wilfully, or elles putteth certeine material thynges in hire secree places to slee the child, or elles dooth unkyndely [unnaturally] synne, by which man or womman shedeth hire nature in manere or in place the as a child may not be conceived, or elles if a woman hae conceyved, and hurt hirself and sleeth the child, yet is it homycide.[10]

Clearly referenced in this excerpt are contraceptive potions (venenouse herbes); abortifacient potions (sleeth the child); the use of abortive instruments (certeine material thynges); *coitus interruptus* (in manere…as a child may not be conceived); anal coitus (or in place…); and abortion (hurt hirself and sleeth the child). As Fryer points out, "all these are equated with murder." While all these practices may well have occurred (though rarely) in Europe during the Middle Ages, Carr-Saunders is of the opinion that other factors (particularly delayed or avoided marriages) adequately explain why the European population did not grow significantly during this time.

But what happened when impediments preventing early marriage were eliminated? Not surprisingly, the population began to grow in nations influenced by Judeo-Christian principles. And grow it did! The population of England and Wales grew from about 4 million people in 1509 to close to 9 million in 1801.[11] The population of the United States (influenced by immigration, as well as having a very high birth rate) grew dramatically, from about 1 million in 1740, to about 5 million in 1800, sixty years later.[12] Similar growth in population can be seen in other European nations between 1500 and 1800, based on the best data available.

This is not to say that techniques to prevent births were not used by certain people during these times. According to Fryer, some Frenchmen publicly advocated the use of birth control devices as early as the 1700s. Fueling this early birth control movement were

---

10. *Works of Chaucer*, ed. Robinson, 1957. Cited in Fryer, 21-22.
11. Carr-Saunders, *Population*, 2–3.
12. Carr-Saunders, *Population*, 24.

a number of factors, such as: (1) the desire to avoid frequent pregnancies, a practice considered unhealthy; (2) the desire to retain health, good looks, and to avoid pain; (3) the goal to ensure that each child could enjoy the best possible food, entertainment, and education; and, perhaps most importantly, what Fryer calls (4) "a marked change in people's attitude to[ward] love." Here Fryer says something about eighteenth-century France that makes us think of modern America: "In the vocabulary of love, and in the way men and women tended to think about love-making, there had appeared a distinction between pleasure and reproduction. Such a differentiation would have been inconceivable in the Middle Ages. *Without it, there could have been no large scale adoption of contraceptive techniques.*"[13]

Making sex an end in itself, and cutting it off from one of God's intended purposes for sex, inevitably lead to the expectation of using contraception.

As such, it should come as no surprise that even the infamous French pornographer Marquis de Sade (1740–1814), from whom we appropriately glean the word "sadist," had more than a passing interest in preventing pregnancy. In a book he authored in 1795, de Sade described three methods of avoiding pregnancy: (1) the vaginal sponge, (2) the condom, and (3) anal coitus.[14]

In marked contrast to France, most Englishmen during the 1700s overwhelmingly viewed the subject of birth control with great repugnance. The occasional English references to the subject during this time universally condemned the practice. One of the most interesting commentaries on birth control was written in 1727 by Daniel Defoe, author of *Robinson Crusoe*. His book on the subject, *Concerning the Use and Abuse of the Marriage Bed*, contained a chapter entitled, "Of Marrying, and then publickly professing to desire they may have no CHILDREN, and of using Means physical or diabolical, to prevent Conception."

---

13. Fryer, *Birth Controllers*, 35–36, emphasis added.
14. Fryer, *Birth Controllers*, 39.

In his book, Defoe equates contraception with abortion: "Taking Physick before-hand to prevent your being with Child...[is] wilful Murther [murder], as essentially and as effectually, as your destroying the Child after it was formed in your Womb."[15] I can almost hear the guffaws from modern thinkers mocking Defoe's almost embarrassing naiveté in medical matters. But I believe his perspective has much merit, if not from a strictly biological perspective, at least from the standpoint of ethics, spiritual attitudes, and ultimate results. Regardless, during his lifetime, Defoe obviously was "preaching to the choir." Most people in his day (in England and in the United States) agreed that children were a blessing, and proved it by having many of them.

However, over time, the number of children born per woman began decreasing. In 1800, the average American woman bore seven children. From that date to the present, with the exception of the Baby Boom bulge between 1947 and 1964, the trend has been decidedly downward. Since 1973, the average American woman has been having less than two children. To look at the facts another way, according to the Census Bureau, in 1790 the average American household contained 5.79 persons. This value has steadily dropped to the point where we now have only 2.75 persons per household.[16] In other words, we now have families less than half as large as families were in 1800, often living in houses far larger than what were available 200 years ago.

One thing that is clear from this data is that nations under the influence of the Judeo-Christian tradition experienced significant population growth prior to 1900, compared to the rest of the world.[17] But it is also true that the number of children born to the average woman, as well as the rate of population increase, began to decline, first in France prior to 1800, and in the United States

---

15. Fryer, *Birth Controllers*, 37
16. *Wall Street Journal*, Oct. 18, 1983.
17. Carr-Saunders, *Population*, 42.

around 1850, and in England around 1875. What explanation can we give for these marked population downturns?

All the authorities I have read confirm the conclusions of Dr. Carr-Saunders, as he attempted to shed light on this important question. After considering all the possibilities, including less frequent intercourse, abortion, infanticide, general infertility, and contraception, Carr-Saunders concluded that expanded contraceptive practices by people—even in the 1800s—best explains the phenomena of reduced births, and the slowing of population growth in France, England, and America.

As the next chapter will summarize, it was during the 1800s that the early "birth control pioneers" began to propagate their message of reducing family size by various means in England and America (with France already endorsing the practice in the previous century). While methods of preventing conception (both superstitious and actual) have been known and practiced for centuries by at least a minority of people, it seems clear that "only within the last century do we find any organized, planned effort to help the masses to acquire a knowledge of contraception."[18]

Many historians trace the modern propagation of birth control in England and America back to the writings of Thomas Robert Malthus (1766–1834). In his bestseller, *An Essay on the Principle of Population* (1798), Malthus stated his basic premise: "I say, that the power of population is infinitely greater than the power of the earth to produce subsistence for man.... Population, when unchecked, increases in a geometrical ratio. Subsistence increases only in an arithmetical ratio. A slight acquaintance with numbers will shew the immensity of the first power in comparison of the second."[19]

The dilemma of mankind, according to Malthus, is that the sex drive inexorably leads to reproduction, which results in an increasingly large number of mouths to feed. Marital bliss, therefore, is

---

18. Himes, *Medical History*, xxxiv–xxxv.

19. Taken from Garrett Hardin, *Population, Evolution and Birth Control* (San Francisco: W. H. Freeman and Company, 1964), 7.

soon replaced by poverty and misery. So a person and a society are logically led to despair. Should a man marry to satisfy his biological desires, with the likelihood of economic hardship? Or should he stoically endure the pressure of his bodily urges, and spurn marriage? Or worse yet, should he succumb to temptation by turning to vice, prostitution, or other immoral outlets, to satisfy his sexual drive, without producing any children that he is legally obligated to feed?

Is not the obvious solution to Malthus's dilemma the ready access to birth control? If a person can have sex without stooping to "vice" or breeding himself to poverty and misery, the problem would immediately be solved. Interestingly, however, Malthus himself shunned the use of birth control devices "with the most marked disapprobation." The reason for his disapproval?

> Both on account of their immorality and their tendency to remove a necessary stimulus to industry. If it were possible for each married couple to limit by a wish the number of their children, there is certainly reason to fear that the indolence of the human race would be very greatly increased; and that neither the population of individual countries, nor of the whole earth, would ever reach its natural and proper extent.[20]

Garrett Hardin notes that in light of Malthus's strong personal opposition to birth control, "it is curious that the birth-control movement that arose in the nineteenth century should have been called 'neomalthusianism,' an identification that must surely have made Malthus turn in his grave."[21]

But ideas have consequences. Malthus struck a receptive nerve in the minds of many people with his seemingly irrefutable argument. Who can question mathematical truth? Man must inevitably breed himself to the point of starvation. Despite Malthus's personal disdain for contraception, one must conclude from the data the

---

20. Joseph A. Banks, *Victorian Values: Secularism and the Size of Families* (London: Routledge and Kegan Paul, 1981), 19–20.

21. Hardin, *Population*, 189.

obvious need for an artificial reproductive "check" (as it was called then) to stave off personal misery and ultimate societal catastrophe.

When we discuss the issue of "overpopulation" later in this section, we will more completely show, very simply, that Malthus was wrong in his underlying assumptions. In fact, even during his own lifetime, when England's population was burgeoning, per capita economic growth was also occurring, in direct contradiction with Malthus's theories: "Unaware of the [scientific-industrial] revolution he was living in, Malthus implied that any increase in the population of his own country in his own time would result in an increase in 'misery and vice.' History mocked him…throughout the nation, population and prosperity increased more or less hand-in-hand for all the years of Malthus's life."[22]

It may come as some surprise that, besides being a celebrated author, Malthus was also an ordained minister. Unfortunately, Malthus was neither the first nor the last man of the cloth to teach unusual ideas that have had a significantly negative impact on our world. A big part of Malthus's problems stem from his apparent lack of knowledge of—and respect for—the infallible Word of God. His ideas flowed largely from his own brain, apart from God's truth. Similarly, Malthus's lifestyle did not reflect a commitment to spiritual priorities either. When he traveled to Scandinavia, ostensibly to study population issues, Malthus wrote more journal entries about the women of that land, "whose clothes did not completely cover them," than of scientific population themes. Also, his personal library "included a rich collection of bawdy plays and stories."[23] While I don't wish to be unduly scandalous here, I do wish to put the man who has given the world its most persistent (though I believe fallacious) argument for birth control in an accurate light. Though a pastor, he was no saint, and quite possibly not even a true follower of Christ.

---

22. Hardin, *Population*, 32–33.
23.William D. Grampp, "Malthus Had an Eye for Sex, If a Sigh for Procreation," *Wall Street Journal*, March 1, 1984.

In addition to Malthus's significant impact on birth control pioneers, he also fueled the anti-biblical ideas of evolutionists Charles Darwin and Alfred Russel Wallace: "In the minds of both Darwin and Wallace, the stimulus that acted as the immediate releaser of the idea of natural selection was the reading of Malthus's *Essay on Population*."[24]

Please allow me again to say that ideas have consequences! But we are primarily interested in Malthus's impact on the mentality and practice of family limitation rather than evolution. To the present day, the ideas engendered by Malthus continue to impact public policy and private action.

Part B: The Growth of Family Planning
In England and America from 1800–2019

Following the teachings of Malthus in the early 1800s, and continuing to the present day, there have been ten birth control "pioneers" who have had a significant impact, not only on the childbearing decisions of individual couples, but also on the population trends of entire nations. If time and space allowed, it would be interesting to study each of these pioneers in depth. We could talk more of Charles Knowlton's hypochondria and his nighttime, secret exhumation of a corpse for curiosity's sake; of Annie Besant's belief that she had been reincarnated 600 previous times, beginning on the Moon in 600,000 B.C.; of Margaret Sanger's desertion of her husband and children, and her relentless pursuit of fame and sensuality; of her advocacy, along with Marie Stopes, of eugenics. But such would consume too much time for our purposes. For those of you wanting more details, I encourage you to read some of the source books used in this study.

As a means of summarizing the lives of these birth control pioneers, note Figure 1 below, which contains the basic information about each person. The data was gleaned largely from two highly respected works in this area: *The Medical History of*

24. Hardin, *Population*, 137.

Contraception[25] by Norman E. Himes, and *The Birth Controllers*[26] by Peter Fryer. Keep in mind that neither Himes nor Fryer is a red-necked, Bible-thumping conservative. Far from it. In fact, it is clear from their writings that neither of them has anything other than contempt for any religious opposition to the birth control movement. Pro-abortionist Alan F. Guttmacher wrote the preface to Himes's book, and Fryer, in his preface, gives credit to a Norma Meacock (a woman, not his wife) who, among other things, was "carrying our daughter."

What should be obvious from Figure 1 is that virtually all the birth control pioneers were anti-Christian or non-Christians. In fact, commentators on the movement see a logical relationship between their religious perspectives and their proclamation of contraceptive practices and thought. McLaren says of the early birth controllers: "[They were] lumped together as propagators of…a system combining blasphemy, atheism, infidelity, adultery, lewdness, removing all moral and religious and legal checks upon human depravity, and leading to a community of property and striking directly at the foundation of civil society."[27]

Fryer summarized his history of birth controllers in his preface by saying:

> With the exception of Marie Stopes (who never quite reconciled herself to the fact), all the leading pioneers of birth control were convinced freethinkers…. Most of their writings on the subject were issued by secularist publishers…. Margaret Sanger, at first a socialist, came to regard family limitation as a panacea. To her British and American forerunners, it was only part of the general struggle against poverty and against religious cant which refused, childishly or prudishly, to countenance realistic solutions to social problems…. Though they did not see themselves primarily as sexual reformers, the birth

---

25. Himes, *Medical History* (New York: Gamut Press, 1963).

26. Peter Fryer, *The Birth Controllers* (New York: Stein and Day, 1966).

27. Angus McLaren, *Birth Control in Nineteenth-Century England* (New York: Holmes and Meier, 1978), 57.

control pioneers were in many respects direct harbingers of the so-called "new morality" of our own day. They believed that sexual relationships between adults should be regulated by human needs, not by religious dogma.... Today [1965], when unmarried women still find it far from easy to obtain contraceptive instruction and equipment, it is salutary to recall that *the birth control movement, throughout the nineteenth century, was part of a vigorous challenge to Christianity and Christian notions of sin.*"[28]

FIGURE 1

NAME	LIVED	NATION	MOST SIGNIFI-CANT ACTION	IMPACT	RELIGIOUS ORIENTATION
Francis Place	1771–1854	England	Passed out hand-bills and books on contraception	Called "father of birth control movement."	Atheistic
Richard Carlile	1790–1843	England	Published *Every Woman's Book or What is Love* (1825)	Was influential in the lives of subsequent leaders.	Atheistic
Robert Dale Owen	1801–1877	U.S.	Published *Moral Physiology or a Brief and Plain Treatise on the Population Question*	Book widely distributed in the U.S.	Agnostic early; became a spiritist.
Charles Knowlton	1800–1850	U.S.	Published *Fruits of Philosophy or the Private Companion of Young Married People* (1832)	Book widely distributed in both U.S and England.	Philisophical materialism.
George Drysdale	1825–1904	England	Published *Elements of Social Science; or Physical, Sexual and Natural Religion* (1854)	Book widely circulated in England.	Natural religion designed to oppose Christianity.

---

28. Fryer, *The Birth Controllers*, 11–12 (emphasis added).

NAME	LIVED	NATION	MOST SIGNIFI-CANT ACTION	IMPACT	RELIGIOUS ORIENTATION
Charles Bradlaugh	1833–1891	England	Published Knowlton's *Fruits of Philosophy* with Annie Besant. Prosecuted for his work.	Great publicity at trial led to wide public interest in contraception	Atheistic
Annie Besant	1847–1933	England	Published Knowlton's *Fruits of Philosophy* with Bradlaugh. Also published her book, *Law of Population*.	Her prosecution also led to publicity for the issue and a downturn of the English population.	Christian, then atheistic, then the occult.
Margaret Sanger	1883–1966	U.S.	Wrote, spoke, and organized about contraception and eugenics.	Planned Parenthood formed; birth control becomes household word.	Atheistic, but dabbled in occult.
Marie Stopes	1880–1958	England	Authored *Married Love* and *Wise Parenthood*. Opened birth control clinics.	Books sold 2 Million copies in 30 years. Great impact on society and church in England.	Mystic. Claims God told her in a vision about proper birth control devices which did not unnaturally block the "divinely inspired mixing of coital fluids."
Paul Ehrlich	1932–	U.S.	Author of *The Population Bomb* (1968)	Book sold 3 Million copies. Profound impact on culture. Big impact on legalizing abortion in 1973.	Agnostic, possibly pantheistic

The impact of these birth control pioneers cannot be overstated. While the early ones (like Francis Place and Richard Carlile) were largely ridiculed by the general public, their persistence and enlistment of others to join them in the work, and carry their ideas on into the future, had a significant effect on population trends in England and the United States. In 1877, there was a notorious trial involving birth controllers Charles Bradlaugh and Annie Besant which markedly raised public consciousness about the availability of birth control. The book they published on the subject, *Fruits of Philosophy*, began to soar in sales once it became officially "banned."

McLaren documents the significant change in average family size and the corresponding use of birth control devices and means around the time of the Bradlaugh-Besant trial.[29]

Number of children produced by marriages that lasted at least 20 years

Marriage occurred in:	Average number of children per woman
1870s	5.8
1890s	4.13
1860s	6.16
1880s	5.3
1915	2.43

Percent of women controlling or attempting to control their fertility

Women born between:	Percent controlling or attempting to control fertility
1831–1845	19.5%
1861–1870	42.7%
1902–1906	72%

As a result of this downturn in population, John W. Taylor, Professor of Gynecology, in a 1904 address to the British Gynaecological Society, lamented: "Instead of the families of six or twelve to eighteen children, we see more often the so-called family of three

---

29. McLaren, *Birth Control*, 11.

or two or one, and that which used to be—and still should be—the highest and noblest function of the married woman, the rearing of sons and daughters to the family, the nation, and the Empire, is very largely handed over to the lower classes…and to the Hebrew and the alien."[30]

A much more recent birth control "pioneer," Paul Ehrlich, author of *The Population Bomb* (1968), has likewise had a profound impact on the childbearing practices of many couples, and the legalization of abortion in 1973. (See more on the overpopulation issue in Chapter 18.)

What about opposition to the birth control movement? Such opposition certainly existed, but ultimately was no match for the other side. I think it would be helpful to briefly examine the opposition as it existed in three areas: (1) the medical profession, (2) the political/governmental realm, and (3) religious organizations.

The medical community's opposition to birth control was short-lived and tentative. Unfortunately, the medical profession is not the only profession where the offer of additional income is sufficient to lure them to compromise their personal convictions about certain issues. Initially, most physicians argued that it was essentially unhealthy for women to prevent conception in artificial ways. When it was later shown that most mechanical birth control devices did not directly appear to be harmful to a woman's health, medical objections began to fade into the background. One of the first pro-birth control physicians to author a medical journal article on the subject hailed from my hometown of Grand Rapids, Michigan. This physician, O. E. Herrick, wrote the article "Abortion and Its Lesson" published in the *Michigan Medicine News* in 1882. In this pioneering article, Dr. Herrick argued that contraception, if widely practiced, would eliminate the need for abortion. While this argument has been offered by various contraception advocates for decades, the truth is that it has never worked, nor will it ever

---

30. Fryer, *Birth Controllers*, 181, quoting Taylor, *British Gynaecological Journal*, (May, 1904): 27–29.

work to eliminate "unwanted" or "unplanned" children. Abortion will continue to be needed to "fix" contraceptive "failures" and other "mistakes" by couples. At any rate, the medical community gradually came to believe in the apparent benefits of contraception in general, and doctors specifically ignored any possible philosophical or religious concerns. By 1933, 88% of physicians surveyed in Michigan (presumably comparable to the data from other states) indicated that they favored birth control. Those few who objected to birth control largely did so on religious or ethical grounds, not for reasons of their patients' health.[31]

Government also played a role in opposing birth control. Standing head and shoulders above other governmental employees was Anthony Comstock, a man who is always described in the vilest terms by pro-birth control historians. Comstock served as a special inspector for the U.S. Post Office Department in the last decades of the 1800s, until his death in 1915. In this capacity, Comstock helped initiate countless prosecutions, which deterred (for a time) the growth of the birth control industry. Listen to Fryer's disdain for Comstock:

> For forty-two years Anthony Comstock's violent and unshakable prejudices stood between the American people and the free dissemination of contraceptive knowledge. Comstock believed the advocates of contraception were doing the devil's work, in the most literal sense.... His hatred of physicians who tried to give advice on family limitation, and of the radicals who championed their right to do so, was not lessened by the close links which existed, in America as in Britain, between the birth control and free thought movements. Infidelity (i.e. atheism) and obscenity occupied the same bed, he declared in a characteristic metaphor.[32]

---

31. Himes, *Medical History*, 306–307.
32. Fryer, *Birth Controllers*, 193.

It took an agitated Margaret Sanger (who said Comstock possessed a "stunted neurotic nature") to eventually garner enough public support to defeat Comstock and his zealous supporters.

While on the subject of governmental opposition to birth control information, I must bring up one of my favorite Americans, the "Rough Rider" himself, Teddy Roosevelt. Roosevelt was never afraid to call something what it was. Regarding birth control, he said those who limited children were committing a crime against the human race. In fact, he called it "race suicide"—a term that was more widely used for a period of time in the early 1900s. Roosevelt strongly favored people being open to having large families, stating, "When quantity falls off, thanks to willful sterility, the quality will go down too. Willful sterility inevitably produces and accentuates every hideous form of vice.… It is itself worse, more debasing, more destructive than ordinary vice. I rank celibate profligacy as not one whit better than polygamy."[33] Isn't it refreshing to get some straight talk from a politician?

With time, of course, vigorous public opponents of birth control, like Anthony Comstock and Teddy Roosevelt, passed off the scene. Nonetheless, remaining in many states were laws disallowing the dissemination of birth control information and materials. However, in 1963, the U.S. Supreme Court performed the *coup de grace* to states' anti-birth control laws in deciding *Griswold v. Connecticut*. It was in this case that Justice William O. Douglas, speaking for a majority of the Court, discovered for the first time a constitutionally based right of privacy, which would take precedence over a state's desire to outlaw the sale and distribution of contraceptive materials. Justice Black's dissent is a classic: he accurately explained why no honest, thinking person could find a substantive right of privacy in our Constitution. Therefore, he argued, the Court didn't really have the power to tell the legislature of Connecticut that they could not pass anti-contraception laws. Unless a real provision of the Constitution was violated, states could pass whatever

---

33. Fryer, *Birth Controllers*, 199.

laws they wish. Despite Black's dissent, a majority of the Court did rule that the Constitution requires a pro-birth control stance; therefore, any governmental interference with the matter is unlawful. I am personally not surprised that, ten years after *Griswold*, the U.S. Supreme Court, using the same legal principles created in *Griswold*, and even quoting from *Griswold*, fashioned the decision of *Roe v. Wade*, known by most readers as the watershed case that gave America abortion-on-demand.[34]

How about the church's opposition to birth control methods and mentality? Charles D. Provan correctly points out in *The Bible and Birth Control*[35] that all the major Protestant theologians of the past (including Calvin, Luther, Wesley, and others) spoke out against birth control activities based on their commentaries on the sin of Onan in Genesis 38.

It was during the first three decades of the twentieth century that the public perception of birth control markedly changed from being a despicable unmentionable to a tolerated reality. In 1908, the Anglican bishops gathered for their Lambeth Conference, and published a detailed statement decrying the evils of artificial birth control methods. They called upon "all Christian people to discountenance the use of all artificial means of restriction [of children] as demoralizing to character and hostile of national welfare."[36] The primary arguments advanced by the churchmen were more secular than biblical: they expressed a concern about the falling birth rate in England, including a eugenic perspective that the "old English speaking stocks" in England and the United States were being replaced by "foreign stocks" with a higher rate of reproduction.

---

34. For a detailed analysis of the Constitutional legal issues in these cases, see my book, *Justice for the Unborn* (Ann Arbor: Servant Press, 1984).

35. Charles D. Provan, *The Bible and Birth Control* (Monongahela, Penn.: Zimmer Printing, 1989).

36. Richard Allen Solloway, *Birth Control and the Population Question in England, 1877–1930* (Chapel Hill, N.C.: University of North Carolina Press, 1982), 99–100.

In supplying their primary argument against birth control, the church leaders presented dubious medical information concerning how birth control was likely to lead to physical and emotional ailments in any couple using it. Rather than dealing with the unspiritual attitudes that underlie the use of artificial (as well as "natural") contraceptives, the bishops argued more in terms of their desire for a nation with "good stock" and healthy parishioners. In fact, the conference specifically gave their approval for couples choosing to prevent conception through the use of "self-denial" during the woman's fertile days of her menstrual cycle. This approved means of birth control was shared with the laity in a 1913 publication released by the Anglicans entitled *The Misuse of Marriage*.

In my opinion, the bishops gave their congregations a very mixed message. In effect they said, "It's okay to restrict your family size for legitimate reasons in legitimate ways; but it's not alright to restrict your family size in other ways." Little wonder an increasing segment of parishioners ignored the church's teaching as time went on. Why did the bishops equivocate on the issue of natural family planning, as we now call it? One reason may well be that the clergymen and their wives at that time were having fewer and fewer children themselves. In 1874, the average Anglican clergyman had 5.2 children, close to the national norm. However, by 1911, the average clergyman had only 2.3 children, significantly below the then national average of 2.8.[37] Obviously, Anglican ministers were using some means of birth control, "natural" or "unnatural." Only Roman Catholic and Jewish families in England were still having large numbers of children at that time.[38]

In 1911, Marie Stopes sent a questionnaire to a few hundred Anglican clergymen regarding their own personal use of birth control. The questionnaire permitted the responses to be returned anonymously. About 200 surveys were returned to Marie with valid responses. The survey showed the obvious: about half of the clergy

37. Soloway, *Birth Control*, 103.
38. Soloway, *Birth Control*, 102, 109, 110.

used *coitus interruptus* and condoms to prevent pregnancy, and many of the other half admitted to using total abstention or the "rhythm" method.[39] So, to the outside world, the church was decrying the evils of birth control, while many church leaders were engaging in the same practices themselves. When hypocrisy occurs in Christian leadership, it is only a matter of time before our entire culture follows suit. Confronted with the growing usage of birth control both within and without its ranks, the Anglican bishops eventually lost the stomach to fight.

While the bishops reasserted their orthodox, official opposition to artificial contraception in 1920, within another ten years the hypocritical balloon finally burst. Prior to the 1930 conference, much "behind the scenes" work had been done on both sides of the issue. Marie Stopes had sent each prelate a copy of her recent release, *Mother England*, consisting of a collection of letters from working class women whose experiences led them to desire birth control. At the conference in 1930, the bishops heard from Dr. Helena Wright, who described the advantages of birth control for the poor.

Thereafter, by a vote of 193 to 67, the bishops adopted a new resolution on marriage and sex. While reemphasizing that the primary purpose of married love was procreation, and the preferred method of child limitation was abstention from sex, nonetheless it conceded, "In those cases where there is such a clearly felt moral obligation to limit or avoid parenthood, and where there is a morally sound reason for avoiding complete abstinence…other methods may be used, provided that this is done in the light of…Christian principles."[40]

The new policy represented a significant divergence from the old rule, in that it permitted family size decisions to be made based on family, economic, and medical reasons, as one's own conscience dictated. Missing is any mention of concern for the fundamental principles of Scripture as to the blessing of children. No mention is made of ability to open and close the womb as God sees fit. Man

39. Soloway, *Birth Control*, 241.
40. Soloway, *Birth Control*, 252.

now autonomously makes his own determination in this eternally significant area "in light of Christian principles." The Lambeth Conference's ultimate capitulation to humanistic principles in this area occurred in 1958 when, "'Family planning'...was eulogized as a desirable strategy of 'responsible parenthood' clearly in harmony with the human values implicit in the sexual union."[41]

Perhaps we might expect this response from the "liberal" Anglican Church, but American evangelical churches have not done much better. The best evidence of our shortcomings in this area can be seen in a symposium organized jointly by the Christian Medical Society and the editors of *Christianity Today* in the late 1960s. The symposium created *A Protestant Affirmation on the Control of Human Reproduction,* which was published, along with some of the proceedings from the symposium, in a book entitled *Birth Control and the Christian.*[42] The *Protestant Affirmation* has sections that make you shake your head in sorrow and bewilderment. See if you can find any immutable biblical principles forming the basis for their comments on contraception:

> The prevention of conception is not in itself forbidden or sinful providing the reasons for it are in harmony with the total revelation of God for married life. Disease, psychological debility, the number of children already in the family, and financial capability are among the factors determining whether pregnancy should be prevented.... Of all the methods of contraception, sterilization presents the most difficult decision because it impairs the creative activity God has given to man and is usually irreversible. Yet there may be times when a Christian may allow himself (or herself) to be sterilized for compelling reasons which outweigh these factors.[43]

Concerning abortion, the Affirmation states:

---

41. Soloway, *Birth Control,* 254.
42. Walter O. Spitzer and Carlyle L. Saylor, eds., *Birth Control and the Christian* (Wheaton, Ill.: Tyndale House Publishers, 1969).
43. Spitzer, *Birth Control,* xxv.

As to whether or not the performance of an induced abortion is always sinful we are not agreed, but about the necessity and permissibility for it under certain circumstances we are in accord…. The [Christian] physician in making a decision regarding abortion should take into account the following principles:…. The Christian physician will advise induced abortion only to safeguard greater values sanctioned by Scripture. These values should include individual health, family welfare, and social responsibility.[44]

What was the reason a group of leading evangelical Christians in 1969 came to these incredible conclusions? At least in part they were prompted by the Malthusian phobia of overpopulation. The last paragraph of the Affirmation is entitled "The Christian in an Over-Populated World." Perhaps this belief in what it calls the "desperate needs" of "nations and peoples" triggered the use of the phrase "social responsibility" as one of the legitimate reasons for abortion. In any event, with Bible-based Christian leaders taking such a weak stand on abortion in 1969, it is not at all surprising our Supreme Court gave us abortion-on-demand only four short years later.

The Roman Catholic Church in England and America held tighter reign over its members for a longer time than did the Protestant church. The size of Catholic families of a given class between 1871 and 1890 was 6.6 people compared to the average of 3.7 for Protestants of the same class. Such significant differences continued for the next few decades. But Catholics ultimately permitted their people the use of "natural" family planning methods and principles, thereby throwing open the gateway to artificial means of contraception, since the latter achieves the same basic goal as the former, but simply in a more high-tech way. Today, Catholics use birth control devices as regularly (if not more so) than non-Catholics, despite the official teachings of the Roman Catholic Church to the contrary.[45]

---

44. Spitzer, *Birth Control*, xxv-xxvi.

45. A relatively recent study showed that about three out of four Protestants (and the same percent of Catholics) use contraception. Also, by 1988, 22% of Catholic women and 21% of Catholic men were sterilized, a significant increase

It is tragic that the church has largely acquiesced to the secular birth control juggernaut by neglecting, or in some cases refusing to base its stand on, eternal biblical principles—choosing rather to rest its arguments on eugenic or medical grounds, or even based on raw pragmatism. Only when the Word of God is placed in authority over our lives do we acquire the insight and motivation to live for God rather than for ourselves. And only then will we find ourselves surprised by the joy of the Lord.

from 1965 when the numbers were less than 7% for each. "Birth Control Practices Vary Little with Faith," *Wall Street Journal*, May 16, 1990.

CHAPTER 18

The Irresponsible Argument

"Isn't it irresponsible and even selfish to bring more children into what everyone knows is an increasingly overpopulated world?"

There are few myths more widely embraced as fact in our time than the myth that the world is bulging at the seams with untold millions of sweaty, smelly, hungry natives eking out their miserable existences, while they mindlessly continue to breed themselves into literal oblivion. Unfortunately, few of us have ever taken the time to check out the actual facts. Should you bother to check out the actual facts of the "overpopulation" issue, you will quickly learn some amazing truths, including the fact that the world is far from full.

E. Calvin Beisner documents this issue conclusively in *Prospects for Growth*. He indicates that, in 1974, *all* human settlements, from tiny tribal encampments to multi-million-person cities, take up "only about 1% of the land surface of the earth."[1] This means that you could fit the entire human race of 7.5 billion people into the state of Texas with its 268,597 square miles of area, and give each man, woman and child over 700 square feet of space to live in.

The next time you fly over the deserts and mountains in America's West, see for yourself if there is any land area left. The rest of the world has similar desolate places. We are very far from being

---

1. E. Calvin Beisner, *Prospects for Growth* (Westchester, Ill.: Crossway Books, 1990), 37.

overcrowded, and any honest scientist will confirm that fact. Not only can the world tolerate more people, in reality it needs more people for proper economic growth and population stability. I know you will find it difficult to believe this last comment, since it flies directly in the face of modern, conventional wisdom. I hope the subparts of this chapter will convince you of the accuracy of this assertion as we consider the scientific and scriptural perspectives of overpopulation.

Part A: Are there Too Many People for God?

A few years ago, when returning home from a speaking engagement in another city, my assigned seat put me next to a distinguished-looking woman in her forties. As we flew, we began to engage in small talk. It turned out she was a pastor's wife traveling to the East on behalf of a mission board for her church. In prior years, she and her husband had been missionaries.

Our conversation drifted to a discussion of our respective families. I mentioned (with my forgivable degree of pride and joy) that my wife and I were the grateful parents of what were then eight children. I'll never forget the woman's response. Almost immediately, her eyes moistened and, choking back the tears, she said she would give anything to have had more children. But, many years before, due to concerns about overpopulation, she and her husband decided it was their Christian duty to have no more than two children. So, after having two children, the couple dutifully submitted to sterilization.

This woman—whom I had never met before—confessed to me that she now felt that this decision regarding sterilization had produced one of the biggest regrets of her Christian life. She was now convinced that sterilization in her case was not consistent with God's revealed will and that she had been totally foolish. I assured her that God *always* meets us at the point of our need. He can use us in life no matter how many mistakes we have made (I can speak first-hand about the truth of this!) I counseled her to encourage other couples in her church not to make the same mistake she and her husband did. She agreed that this was her desire.

Clearly, this "boogie-man" of overpopulation is no mere theoretical idea; it has significantly impacted many lives, including many Christians who really should have known better. In reality, however, Christians should not be misled by the myth of overpopulation. The Bible speaks unequivocally that overpopulation (in the sense that we have too many people for the resources available on the earth) is not the primary issue that mankind must grapple with. I know this assertion seems almost irresponsible to some, but let me support my premise.

All of us are probably very familiar with God's injunction to Adam and Eve: Then God blessed them, and God said to them, "Be fruitful and multiply; fill the earth and subdue it; have dominion over the fish of the sea, over the birds of the air, and over every living thing that moves on the earth" (Gen. 1:28).

Similarly God said to Noah after the flood: "Be fruitful and multiply, and fill the earth" (Gen. 9:1). And again, "And as for you, be fruitful and multiply; bring forth abundantly in the earth and multiply in it" (Gen. 9:7).

If "breeding ourselves into oblivion" comes as naturally to people as the doomsayers suggest, why did God feel compelled to consistently exhort our ancestors (and through them, us) to multiply and fill the earth? For some of us, our natural inclination is *not* to have children. There is pain, expense, work, and uncertainty involved in the process of bearing and raising children. Having a child should be an act of faith, courage, and selflessness; God's people are to put God's will above their own. Only after we obey do we see *why* God's way is ultimately the best—even if it involves self-sacrifice. God alone knows the future and understands (far better than we can) that mankind is always just one generation away from extinction. In fact, the Bible teaches that ultimately under-population, not over-population, will be the biggest problem for mankind. Listen to Isaiah describing the days before Christ's second coming:

> Behold, the LORD makes the earth empty and makes it waste; distorts its surface and scatters abroad its inhabitants.... The land shall be entirely emptied and utterly plundered (Isa. 24:1, 3).

Why will God do this?

> The earth is also defiled under its inhabitants, because they have transgressed the laws, changed the ordinance, broken the everlasting covenant. Therefore the curse has devoured the earth, and those who dwell in it are desolate. Therefore the inhabitants of the earth are burned, and few men are left (Isa. 24: 5–6).

God may well use famine as well as other "natural" calamities to destroy the people of the world in the last days, but the reason He will do so relates to the *spiritual condition* of the earth's inhabitants, not their victimization by "overpopulation." No amount of birth control will be able to save the earth's inhabitants from God's judgment in those days. Only righteousness will.

One of the clearest teachings of Scripture is that God will care for His people as they obey Him. Another portion of Isaiah teaches this:

> "I am the LORD your God, who teaches you to profit, who leads you by the way you should go. Oh, that you had heeded My commandments! Then your peace would have been like a river, and your righteousness like the waves of the sea. Your descendants also would have been like the sand; and the off-spring of your body like the grains of sand; his name would not have been cut off nor destroyed from before Me" (Isa. 48:17–19).

Then God gives a reminder of how He did care for His people:

> [The Israelites] did not thirst when He led them through the deserts; He caused the water to flow from the rock for them; He also split the rock, and the waters gushed out (Isa. 48:21).

Imagine more than two million people wandering through a vast desert wilderness unable to utilize modern agricultural methods. Humanly speaking, these people were doomed: it is the classic overpopulation scenario. But God is not dead! He cared for His people and gave them food and water to sustain them. They perished only when they disobeyed God. Is that merely an Old Testament concept? Or are Christians in our day able to ask God for their provisions in the face of an uncertain world? Without a doubt, we Christians today should expect that our heavenly Father will meet all of our needs. Jesus encouraged us to pray, "Give us day by day our daily bread" (Luke 11:3).

Jesus spent much time emphasizing that we are not to worry about food and clothing because our heavenly Father knows our needs and will meet those needs. Our top goal must be to trust and obey: "But seek first the kingdom of God and His righteousness, and all these things [including food, drink, and clothing] shall be added to you" (Matt. 6:33).

To conclude, no Christian who reads and believes his or her Bible should be fooled by the overpopulation myth. It should not be surprising that the scholars who have honestly and thoroughly researched the issue end up supporting God's view in Scripture that the sky is *not* falling, that the world *never* will be really over-populated in terms of not having the capacity to feed and clothe its inhabitants. Shortages will occur because of man's *spiritual* condi-tion, not because we have too many people.

Before we get into scientific specifics, it might be helpful to describe the philosophical contrasts between the gloom-mongers on the one hand, and the growing number of scholars on the other who are optimistic about population growth in the world.

Part B: Malthus's Ideas are Alive and Well

In essence, there are two basic schools of thought throughout history relating to this issue of overpopulation. One perspective is that man must endlessly fret and worry about where tomorrow's meal will be coming from. While those holding this view may be "believers," the "god" they worship is neither loving nor powerful. I don't mean to imply that we are not to work, and even work hard to put food on our tables. But there is no place for endless worry for the child of God: "The LORD is my shepherd; I shall not want" (Ps. 23:1).

The other fundamental point of view holds to the conviction that we have a heavenly Father who watches over us, cares for us, and will meet all our needs. While the first way of thinking blocks out trust in God, the second way of thinking trusts God to meet our needs.

An examination of the history of the birth control movement in our culture reveals the prevalence of the unbelieving attitude in most of the early birth control pioneers. Beginning with Thomas Malthus, all the pioneers of birth limitation felt that, without birth control, man is destined to eke out his meager existence at the mercy of impersonal mathematical realities.

A loving, powerful God is nowhere to be found in the world-view of these birth control pioneers. Tragically, in the early 1900s, some segments of the organized church began also to accept this pessimistic Malthusian thinking, with the ultimate result that birth control and abortion began to be gradually viewed as "responsible" Christianity—and the world has been attempting to squeeze us into its mold ever since.

This debate between these two alternative positions—between a living and loving God on one hand, and a dead or uncaring God on the other, continues to the present day. On the side of Malthus we have gloom-mongers like Dr. Paul Ehrlich, author of the widely read essay, *The Population Bomb*;[2] Dennis Meadows, co-author of *The Limits to Growth*; Dr. Gerald O. Barney, study director of the

---

2. Paul Ehrlich, *The Population Bomb* (New York: Ballantine Books, 1968).

Global 2000 Report to the President; former Colorado Governor Richard "Governor Gloom" Lamm; as well as organizations such as The World Bank and the Rockefeller Foundation.

On the side of hopefulness, we have such people as Dr. Julian Simon, author of *The Ultimate Resource* and *The Resourceful Earth*; Ben Wattenberg, author of *The Good News is the Bad News is Wrong*[3] and *The Birth Dearth*; Colin Clark, author of *The Myth of Overpopulation*;[4] Dr. Rousas J. Rushdoony, author of another book also entitled *The Myth of Overpopulation*;[5] and an excellent book by E. Calvin Beisner called *Prospects for Growth: A Biblical View of Population, Resources, and the Future.*[6]

Throughout our history, there have been certain pamphlets or books that have ignited public attitudes and thoughts in a significant way. We think of Thomas Paine's *Common Sense*, which rallied people to the cause of the Revolutionary War movement in the mid-1700s. Similarly, Harriet Beecher Stowe's *Uncle Tom's Cabin* marshaled much enthusiasm for the anti-slavery movement in the 1850s.

Regarding overpopulation, it was Paul Ehrlich's book, *The Population Bomb*, that ignited society's near panic about the excessive amount of people in our world. This book moved us to consider the need for drastic measures (like free access to birth control and therapeutic abortions) to permit the human race to survive into the future. Writing from a pseudo-scientific perspective, Ehrlich attempts to document his claim that "The battle to feed all of humanity is over."[7] He soon tips his hand as to where he stands

---

3. Ben Wattenberg, *The Good News is the Bad News is Wrong* (New York: Simon and Schuster, 1984).

4. Colin Clark, *The Myth of Overpopulation* (Houston, Tex.: Lumen Christi Press, 1975).

5. Rousas J. Rushdoony, *The Myth of Overpopulation* (Nutley, N.J.: Craig Press, 1969).

6. E. Calvin Beisner, *Prospects for Growth: A Biblical View of Population, Resources, and the Future* (Westchester, Ill.: Crossway Books, 1990).

7. Ehrlich, *Population Bomb*, Prologue.

philosophically and religiously: "The urge to reproduce has been fixed in us by billions of years of evolution."[8]

One of the more unintentionally humorous parts of Ehrlich's monologue is the chapter entitled, "The Ends of the Road."[9] In this chapter, Ehrlich paints a vivid word picture of alternative destinies awaiting us based on our current choices as a people. Patronizingly, Ehrlich assures us how much better things will go if we are willing to heed his gloom and doom warnings and comply with his "scientific" suggestions. While he obviously was dead serious in making his predictions, they look laughable from our perspective today.

In the scenario Ehrlich feels most likely to happen if his recommendations are not followed, he gives a grim prophecy of what life in the United States will be like in 1979 (the book was written in 1968):

1. "The last non-Communist government in Latin America, that of Mexico, is replaced by a Chinese-supported military junta."

2. "Famine has swept repeatedly across Asia, Africa, and South America."

3. 65% of the starving Egyptian population is killed by a "particularly virulent strain of bubonic plague."

4. "In 1977...India fell apart into a large number of warring minor states."

5. "In the United States there is actually less meat to eat than at any stage in our history.... Food and water rationing are standard."

6. "The third Los Angeles killer smog in two years has wiped out 90,000 people."

7. "The President's Environmental Advisory Board...recommends the immediate compulsory restriction of births

---

8. Ehrlich, *Population Bomb*, 29.
9. Ehrlich, *Population Bomb*, 69.

to one per couple, and compulsory sterilization of all persons with I.Q. scores under 90. It says that, unless the population size in the United States is reduced rapidly, it too will be facing massive famine by the year 2000."

8. "Pollution and pesticide poisonings have supplanted cardio-vascular disease as the number one killer of Americans."

9. "In early 1980...in the United States, right-wing pressure to launch preemptive nuclear strikes against both China and Russia became extreme. Sino-Russian intelligence estimating that the President will yield to pressure, recommends a first strike by Communist forces...and a general thermonuclear war ensues."

10. "Small pockets of *Homo sapiens* hold on for awhile in the Southern Hemisphere, but slowly die out."

11. "The most intelligent creatures ultimately surviving this period are cockroaches."[10]

Ehrlich's predictions, which influenced millions of Americans at the time to live in fear, makes me think of the current dire warnings we are hearing about how Climate Change (also called Global Warming) will destroy mankind within twelve years. Fear is a motivator, especially if it is far enough into the future that it can neither be proven nor refuted.

Clearly Ehrlich was totally wrong in his prognostications. We have a glut of food in this country, and there has been an increase in the amount of food produced, even in places like India. Famines have occurred in certain parts of Africa, but as we shall see in subsequent material, the real culprit behind this devastation has not been due to drought, or too many people in the land, as much as it has been due to governmental neglect and incompetence.

At any rate, after painting this dire picture of life in a hopelessly overcrowded world, Ehrlich benevolently shares with us mere

---

10. Ehrlich, *Population Bomb*, 69–78.

mortals his brilliant strategy to avert the catastrophe just described. He says the answer is "simple": "We must rapidly bring the world population under control, reducing the growth rate to zero or making it go negative. Conscious regulation of human numbers must be achieved."[11] Ehrlich feels the U.S. must take the lead in reducing world population by bringing our own population size under control. "We want our propaganda [to be] based on 'do as we do'—not 'do as we say.'"[12]

To regulate our births, Ehrlich recommends governmental compulsory birth regulations: "One plan often mentioned involves the addition of temporary sterilants to water supplies or staple food. Doses of the antidote would be carefully rationed by the government to produce the desired population size."[13] Ehrlich concedes that people would probably resist such a plan, so he recommends instead a tax incentive to encourage "reproductive responsibility." He recommends much higher taxes for people with more children than those with less. He also feels there should be "luxury taxes" imposed on layettes, cribs, diapers, and diaper service. On top of this should be the giving of governmental prizes or grants to couples who delay marriage, undergo sterilization, or who have less than two children.[14]

Ehrlich further recommends the legalization of abortion and the teaching of sex education in schools, including the techniques of birth control. The utopia that will result when we follow his strategy sounds a lot like the rhetoric of other birth control pioneers we have met earlier in this book:

> If we take proper steps in education, legislation, and research, we should be able in a generation to have a population thoroughly enjoying its sexual activity, while raising smaller numbers of physically and mentally healthier children. The population should be relatively free of the horrors created today by divorce,

---

11. Ehrlich, *Population Bomb*, 131.
12. Ehrlich, *Population Bomb*, 135.
13. Ehrlich, *Population Bomb*, 135.
14. Ehrlich, *Population Bomb*, 138.

illegal abortion, venereal disease, and the psychological pressures of a sexually repressive and repressed society.[15]

Since the publication of *The Population Bomb*, the birth rate in the United States has fallen to below replacement levels. As we will see in the next section, this means a population *decline* as the large group of baby boomers moves into the "sunset" years and are replaced by a smaller group of parents bearing smaller numbers of children.

In a real sense, Paul Ehrlich and his compatriots have won a major victory: our society now has significantly reduced its birth rates and has legalized abortion as well, all in keeping with Ehrlich's prescriptions. So where is the utopia he promised? Where are these happily married, sexually contented, healthy people? Why are we plagued with sexually transmitted diseases unheard of in 1968 that have been literally killing growing segments of the world's population?

Isn't it clear that when we leave God out of the picture, we *always* harm ourselves? And Ehrlich definitely does leave God out of the picture. Toward the end of *The Population Bomb*, Ehrlich again betrays his religious convictions. After condemning the Judeo-Christian tradition as essentially inimical to our ecosystem due to an attitude which dominates and exploits nature, Ehrlich speaks wistfully of a bygone era when man worshiped the spirits of trees, springs, hills, and streams. He feels we should learn from the hippie movement which (he says) is devoted to good things like "Zen Buddhism, physical love, and a disdain for material wealth."[16]

As we shall see, it's not difficult to find major flaws in the reasoning contained in *The Population Bomb*. But deception has power just as the truth does. Just as truth sets us free, lies have the power to enslave us. And much of the damage has already been done! God alone knows how many people like the pastor's wife I described at the start of this chapter have been led astray by the lies contained in *The Population Bomb*. My guess is that millions of Americans and probably many more elsewhere have limited their numbers of

15. Ehrlich, *Population Bomb*, 141.
16. Ehrlich, *Population Bomb*, 171.

children as a direct or indirect result of Ehrlich's bold yet devious arguments. It's high time we expose the deception and replace it with the truth.

Another book that has played a significant role in communicating to our culture that a major catastrophe from the existence of too many people lurks just around the corner is *The Limits to Growth* by Donella H. Meadows, Dennis L. Meadows, Jorgen Randers, and William W. Behrens III. Published in 1972, this book sold more than four million copies worldwide and was widely publicized in the media due to its aura of scientific plausibility.

Providentially, I have had more than a passing familiarity with the material contained in *The Limits to Growth*. Dennis Meadows, the primary author (despite giving his wife, Donella, priority on the book jacket), was a young Associate Professor at M.I.T. when I was a Teaching Assistant there, both of us having duties in the same area of learning. I knew Dennis fairly well at M.I.T. as we both worked with our mentor, Professor Jay W. Forrester, who had invented a powerful computer simulation technology known as "System Dynamics" which was used by Meadows in *The Limits to Growth*.

Without getting too deeply into what System Dynamics is, I do want you to understand a little of why I feel the conclusions of *Limits* are not to be embraced with awe. As the title implies, *The Limits to Growth* advocates a shift of thinking from "growth is good" to "enough is enough." Meadows begins his second chapter, "The Limits to Exponential Growth," with quoting Luke 14:28, "For which of you, intending to build a tower, sitteth not down first, and counteth the cost, whether he have sufficient to finish it?" He then attempts to prove how natural resources and food production are necessarily limited by some unknown but absolute value. And who can escape this logic: when the refrigerator is empty, it's empty! Doesn't the same logic apply to our world as a whole?

We shall see in the next section the surprising answer to this question. Not only is the world's "refrigerator" *not* empty, it need *never* be considered empty. Temporary limitations and shortages can actually be the incentive mankind uses to seek and find new sources of food and other needed resources.

Nonetheless, Meadows concludes his "Limits" chapter with the seemingly reasonable (though I believe erroneous) conclusion: "By now it should be clear that all of these tradeoffs arise from one simple fact—the earth is finite" (p. 93). His view of the finiteness of the world, and the inability of technology to eliminate seemingly absolute "Limits to Growth," logically leads Meadows to a predictable conclusion: If the world is limited in its "carrying capacity," and if the explosive growth of population is inevitable, we "worldlings" have a devastating catastrophe staring us in the face, be it by starvation or pollution or some other means.

Clearly Meadows's presuppositions lead inexorably to his conclusions. Meadows's computer model of the world paints with a very broad brush. He attempts to approximate all the essential happenings in the world in less than one hundred variables, which are interconnected with "feedback loops" or the flow of information. You might say it's quite a simplification of what really goes on in the world!

I personally feel that System Dynamics is an excellent tool for understanding complex systems. But there are certain inherent limitations in its use that cannot be ignored:

1. By necessity, System Dynamics oversimplifies all complex social systems. As such, the model builder must exercise significant discretion and judgment in choosing the variables he will include in his model versus the ones he will choose to disregard.

2. System Dynamics models are by definition secularistic: they assume social systems are *closed* with no possibility of any miraculous input from God (like feeding Elijah with meat and bread "airmailed" by way of ravens, or feeding millions of Israelites for forty years with manna).

One distinct advantage of System Dynamics models, however, is that the modelers' assumptions are clear for everyone to see, and therefore all assumptions used can be easily changed to show what impact something would have on the results. Output from System Dynamics models is in the form of computer-generated graphs and tables, which can then be studied in detail. In Meadows's World Model, catastrophic results logically flow from his initial assumptions—especially the belief that as we "run out" of resources, the cost of developing new ones increases dramatically, consuming inordinate amounts of capital.

If you assume, however, that technology (and divine providence) will allow non-renewable resources to be obtained for about the same cost per unit as in the past (which, we will soon see, is the truth), the system continues to show sustained growth instead of catastrophe.[17] Hence, despite my personal appreciation for Dennis Meadows as a person, his model is of little benefit for those of us who know that the Malthusian view of the world is wrong. As with all computer programs, the GIGO (Garbage In, Garbage Out) principle still applies. A computer does not sanitize erroneous assumptions.

Receiving similarly wide exposure has been the *Global 2000 Report to the President*, prepared under the direction of another person I have personally worked with, Dr. Gerald O. Barney.[18] So that you can understand the connection, Dr. Barney was at M.I.T. as a graduate student learning the methodology of Systems Dynamics under Professor Jay W. Forrester alongside *Limits to Growth* author Dennis Meadows (and, somewhat earlier, myself).

While I didn't know Dr. Barney when I was a student at M.I.T., I met him when I was on active duty in the Navy and, in fact, was assigned temporarily to work with him during his employment at the Center for Naval Analyses (CNA). Gerald Barney has sincerely attempted to integrate his religious beliefs into world ecological

---

17. H.S.D. Cole, ed., *Models of Doom* (New York: Universe, 1973), 130.
18. *Global 2000 Report to the President*, 3 vols. (Washington D.C.: Government Printing Office, 1982).

policy. I admire him for his consistency and caring. However, I respectfully disagree with his methodology and conclusions.

Dr. Barney was the Study Director for the *Global 2000 Report*, prepared for President Carter in 1982. The primary governmental agencies involved in this project were the Department of State and the Council on Environmental Quality (CEQ). In addition, other agencies cooperated in the study, including the Departments of Agriculture, Energy, and Interior, the Agency for International Development (AID), the Central Intelligence Agency (CIA), the Environmental Protection Agency (EPA), the Federal Energy Management Agency, the National Aeronautics and Space Administration (NASA), the National Science Foundation, the National Oceanic and Atmospheric Administration, and the Office of Science and Technology Policy.[19]

Including these high-level professionals on the study committee should have ensured that the group's conclusions would be above reproach. Unfortunately, even a simple reading of the report leads one to question the reliability of its conclusions. And a person will become even more skeptical after reading the penetrating work of Dr. Julian Simon and others in *The Resourceful Earth*, a book written to refute the conclusions of *Global 2000*.

The first sentences in the Executive Summary of the *Global 2000 Report* tell us succinctly what the lengthy report concludes:

> If present trends continue, the world in 2000 will be more crowded, more polluted, less stable ecologically, and more vulnerable to disruption than the world we live in now. Serious stresses involving population, resources, and environment are clearly visible ahead. Despite greater material output, the world's people will be poorer in many ways than they are today.[20]

With this as their departure point, the authors of the *Global 2000 Report* attempt to support their perspective that we are heading

19. *Global 2000 Report*, vol. 1: v.
20. *Global 2000 Report*, vol. 1: 1.

inexorably for bleak days in the future. The underlying data, however, can also be used to support a much more optimistic conclusion of things than *The Resourceful Earth* methodically details (but more on that later).

What is essential to note now is the correlation between Barney's work and that of Meadows in *Limits to Growth*. In Volume 2 of *Global 2000*, Dr. Barney spends much time examining what he considered to be some serious shortcomings of Meadows's World Model. Despite his criticism, however, Barney still chose to embrace the Model's basic conclusion that we face virtual extinction as a human race if we do not reverse our stampede for economic and population growth soon.

As with anyone's work, we can obtain significant insights into Barney's mind if we know more about his underlying personal beliefs. Fortunately for us, Dr. Barney has written a thought-provoking article on his view of the connection between Christian theology and the ecology of our world. Entitled, *The Future of the Creation: The Central Challenge for Theologians,*[21] Barney's article suggests that the significant problems facing mankind (including poverty, pollution, injustice, population growth, depletion of resources, fear, hatred, greed, etc.) arise from our faulty "vision of the future of the creation." He encourages the church to lead mankind in providing a vision for the future that will preserve creation.

Barney feels our present "great vision guiding human affairs" is one of "prosperity through industrial development and a demographic transition, and security through violence (or the threat of violence)." Barney says this growth mentality has failed us since, with the depletion of irreplaceable energy reserves and the consequent rising costs, underdeveloped nations will find it next to impossible to develop as we have done. From a theological perspective, Dr. Barney says, "There is an inherent tension or conflict between the biblical injunction to 'Be fruitful and multiply; fill the

---

21. Gerald Barney, "The Future of the Creation: The Central Challenge for Theologians," *World and Word*, vol. 4, no. 4.

earth…' (Gen. 1:28) and to '…tend and keep it' (Gen. 2:15)."[22] His answer? Dr. Barney suggests we adopt a new view of the future by looking to Romans 6:1–4. In this passage, Paul reminds us that as Christ died and was raised from the dead, we theologically did the same, with the goal being that "we also should walk in newness of life" (Rom. 6:4).

While this passage clearly refers to the individual Christian striving to live a righteous life for God in a fallen world, Dr. Barney wonders whether this principle of new life could not also be applied to all of creation. That is, could not Christians offer a "new life" view of the universe, which would ultimately lead to sustaining it rather than pushing it toward its ultimate destruction and death? Dr. Barney seems to think so. He encourages theologians to lead the way by offering a new vision of the future that will help sustain the creation. A top priority, he feels, is to address a serious threat to creation which is, "The conflict between human fruitfulness and the necessity to cultivate and take care of the creation."[23] So, in his view, God would have Christians accept the fact that growth cannot go on forever, and that equilibrium or status quo should become our goal.

I would respond in three ways:

(1) Barney's application of Romans 6 is, at best, unconvincing. Scripture must not be taken out of context nor made to conflict with other scriptures. To conclude from Romans 6 that overpopulation is something that should be opposed, especially in light of other scriptures to the contrary, is wrong.

(2) As stated elsewhere in this book, God seems to love to see His people thrive and grow in numbers. He who feeds the sparrows is never worried about finding enough food to feed us. The real destroyer of God's people and their temporal happiness is not their childbearing. It is violating God's clear commands in Scripture.

---

22. Barney, *Future of Creation*, 423.
23. Barney, *Future of Creation*, 428.

(3) Believe it or not, the actual evidence shows that more people on earth means a higher standard of living *per capita* in the long run than fewer people. In the next section, we will examine why this is true.

This pessimistic view that man is inexorably heading toward misery is a theme that Satan has been peddling on us since the dawn of time. The "missionaries" of this doom and gloom gospel speak with impeccable credentials—even as Malthus did in the early 1800s.

Part C: Why More People are Not the Problem But Can Actually be the *Solution*!

With most of us living at a time when mostly unquestioned conventional wisdom instructs us that many of the knotty problems of our world are a direct or indirect result of overpopulation, it is difficult for us to imagine a time when most thinking people felt just the opposite. This historical fact is well documented by Austrian-born Joseph A. Schumpeter, whose distinguished academic career in economics ultimately brought him to Harvard University where he remained until his death in 1950.

Called "our century's greatest economic historian and one of the greatest economists" by the *Wall Street Journal*,[24] Schumpeter tells us that in the 1600s and 1700s "governments began to favor increase in population by all means at their commands." Until approximately 1750 they viewed a "numerous and increasing population...[as] the most important *symptom* of wealth; it was the chief *cause* of wealth; it *was* wealth itself—the greatest asset for any nation to have."[25] Schumpeter makes it clear he agrees with the idea that wealth flows from a growing population: "Under prevailing conditions, increase

---

24. Robert L Bartley, "Time to Shake Our Hypochondria," *Wall Street Journal*, January 2, 1990.

25. Joseph A. Shumpeter, *History of Economic Analysis* (New York: Oxford University Press, 1954), 251.

in heads would increase real income per head."[26] Because Schumpeter believed this perspective to be "manifestly correct," he found it initially difficult, as an historian, to explain why "the opposite attitude—Malthusian—should have asserted itself among economists from the middle of the eighteenth century on. *Why was it that economists took fright at a scarecrow!*"[27]

Indeed. Why would Malthusianism, the pessimistic view that a growing population leads to significant want, grow in prevalence during the great Industrial Revolution—a time of population growth? Schumpeter seeks an answer to this question from the French experience. He states that in France, which he calls the "cradle" of the "anti-population doctrine," there was a growing economic pessimism because its monarchical form of government (among other factors) "was not favorable to vigorous economic development at home."[28]

As to why England, which was growing by leaps and bounds in both population and per capita income, should become sympathetic to Malthus's pessimistic teachings, Schumpeter is of the opinion that short-run problems always accompany a time of economic growth. The faster the growth, the more intense the short-run problems (e.g., unemployment), particularly when a culture is moving from agriculture, as the principal industry, to manufacturing:

> In the Industrial Revolution of the last decades of the eighteenth century, these short-run vicissitudes grew more serious than they had been before, precisely because the pace of economic development quickened. And some economists—a minority only—were so impressed by them as to lose sight of the trend. The resulting anti-populationist mood then produced the set of propositions that came to be known as the Malthusian principle or theory of population.[29]

---

26. Shumpeter, *Economic Analysis*, 251–52.
27. Shumpeter, *Economic Analysis*, 252, emphasis added.
28. Shumpeter, *Economic Analysis*, 252.
29. Shumpeter, *Economic Analysis*, 252.

Picking up on Schumpeter's theme are a number of people, the most notable of which is Dr. Julian Simon, a professor of economics at the University of Maryland. To read even the claims on the cover of one of Dr. Simon's fascinating books, *The Ultimate Resource*, makes you wonder if he sells snake oil in his spare time. Here are some of them:

- Natural resources and energy are getting *less* scarce.
- Pollution in the U.S. has been decreasing.
- The world's food supply is improving.
- Population growth has long-term benefits.

Accustomed as we are to hearing bad news, we instinctively reject such optimism in skeptical disbelief as we read this litany of Pollyannaish statements. But I assure you that Julian Simon's books are not mere intellectual pipe dreams. Indeed, his logic and data, when studied, will ultimately arm-wrestle you into submission.

Simon has not always been on the optimistic side of the population issue. As an economist, he initially approached the study of "overpopulation" assuming "that the accepted view [of the issue] was sound." In his own words,

> I aimed to help the world contain its exploding population, which I believed to be one of the two main threats to mankind (war being the other). But my reading and research led me into confusion. Though the standard economic theory of population (which has hardly changed since Malthus) asserts that a higher population growth implies a lower standard of living, the available empirical data do not support that theory. My technical book [*The Economics of Population Growth*], which is the predecessor of this volume, is an attempt to reconcile that contradiction. It leads to a theory that suggests population growth has positive economic effects in the long run, though there are costs in the short run.[30]

---

30. Julian L. Simon, *The Ultimate Resource* (Princeton: Princeton University Press, 1981), 9.

Simon's basic point is consistent with Schumpeter's premise: while a child is a short-term expense to a family and society, in the long run, that same child will be able to give back to the world considerably more than he or she consumes. People are not merely mouths to feed. They are individuals with intelligence, creativity, and resourcefulness that can give more than they take. Christian author and scholar E. Calvin Beisner documents the economic value of a person in *Prospects for Growth*. He states:

> The simple economic truth is that, on the average, people are worth more than they cost—about 13.5 times more for males and 6.5 times more for females (figuring solely on the basis of measurable economic income, not including the tremendous value of the financially unpaid work people—especially women—perform at home).[31]

Christian author Rousas J. Rushdoony provides us with a helpful historical illustration of this point. He describes how, before the arrival of the white man, the approximately 250,000 American Indians living in North America faced a continuing problem of "overpopulation" as they hunted for the food to keep them alive. Humanly speaking, the arrival of thousands of white colonists should have exacerbated the problem. Instead, "The coming of the white man increased the food supply, because the white man developed the earth."[32] Rushdoony points out that "some counties in California today produce more food than perhaps the Indians of North, South, and Central America ever saw in a year."[33]

Assume we still had only 250,000 people in the continental United States. What time-saving conveniences (we now consider necessities) would we have? Would we still be cooking food over an open fire, driving horse-drawn wagons, using horse-drawn plows, and living in hand-built homes without running water? While such a thought can produce pleasant feelings in us reminiscent of *Little*

---

31. Beisner, *Prospects for Growth*, 52.
32. Rushdoony, *Myth of Overpopulation*, 3.
33. Rushdoony, *Myth of Overpopulation*, 3.

House on the Prairie, the reality is, in such a situation we would be forced to spend most of our human energy merely keeping "soul and body together." Many more of us would need to return to agriculture as our principal occupation. Would our per capita standard of living be higher in that situation than today with well over one thousand times more people? By no means! People themselves have brought progress.

The fact is, Malthus did not accurately explain the way God has made the universe. As our country has grown, God has put it in the minds of great inventors and businessmen to develop methods and devices which make our lives more effective and increase our per capita standard of living at a rate faster than our population growth. For the past one hundred years, America's economic growth has averaged 3.3% per year, while our population has grown by only 1.5% per year. Japan and Germany have experienced similar increases.[34]

Not only does Julian Simon recount how Malthusians have disregarded our country's ultimate resource—our imaginative people—he also provides another reason why the Malthusians are wrong: they assume the world is essentially a closed system with finite limits. In reality, the world should be viewed as being *open*, with no practical limits. We can all easily comprehend the concept of running out of a given resource in the short run. But this is really a very narrow-minded and short-term view of the issue. The big picture perspective is to look at the situation from a broader perspective and see how a short-term lack can actually turn into a long-term gain.

It obviously makes for more interesting news for media to describe a "crisis" in the apparent lack of a critical resource than to bore us with the news of how things are really improving in the long run. Special-interest groups have been formed for no reason other than to inform us of the impending loss of scarce resources such as

---

34. Lester C. Thurow, "Why the Ultimate Size of the World's Population Doesn't Matter," *Technology Review*, August/September, 1986, 22.

clean air, or elephant tusks, or natural gas, or whatever, but no one spends the time telling us that in the long run things are actually getting better. In an abbreviated *Wall Street Journal* essay, Simon states his major thesis:

> Evidence shows that, given some time to adjust to shortages with known methods and new inventions, free people create additional resources confuting Malthusian reasoning. The extraordinary aspect of this process that begins with actual or perceived shortages due to population or income growth is that it eventually leaves us better off than if the shortage had never arisen, thanks to resulting new techniques. Plastics, for example, began as a substitute for elephant ivory in billiard balls after tusks began to grow scarce.[35]

In *The Ultimate Resource*, Simon provides other helpful illustrations of this thesis. For example, he describes how, years ago, everyone had to have a copper pot for cooking. As the demand for copper pots grew, the readily available supply of copper dwindled, and the cost of copper increased. In reality, we don't really care whether our cooking pots are made of copper as long as they function as well as copper pots did. Soon iron and steel began to be used to replace copper in pots, and now we can buy the equivalent of a copper pan for far less than that pan would be if it was made out of copper. Man's mind, prompted by a temporary shortage, designed an improvement. Beyond that, Simon suggests:

> We want intercontinental telephone and television communication, and, as long as we can get it, we do not care whether this requires 100,000 tons of copper for [underwater] cables or just a single quarter-ton communication satellite in space that uses no copper at all.[36]

See the picture? When man is free to respond to temporary shortages, the net result can often be overall improvement.

---

35. Julian Simon, "Myths of Overpopulation," *Wall Street Journal*, August 3, 1984.

36. Simon, *Ultimate Resource*, 46.

While I agree with Simon's basic premise, I personally believe it breaks down at a certain point. In short, Simon seems to disregard the "sin factor." If man were not sinful, Simon's recipe for human progress would always work: in all cases, simply turn people loose to solve the problems they face. But you can't permit self-centered people to have too much freedom, since, if they refuse to govern themselves, they will soon begin to devour each other in their freedom. But truly self-governing people, with moral standards they adhere to, can be given a lot of freedom, which, I am convinced, is the ideal environment for economic growth in the long run. This has been the source of America's rich heritage. It is a fair question, however, whether, apart from a renewed spiritual awakening, with its attendant diligence and selflessness, we will continue to experience such blessings into the future.

Simon's other significant book, *The Resourceful Earth*[37] (co-authored with Herman Kahn), is a specific scholarly response to the *Global 2000 Report* to the President. *The Resourceful Earth* describes in elaborate detail how the world is improving, and that it is not relentlessly moving us toward an ecological catastrophe—nor are we running out of "non-renewable" resources. Again, Simon's logic and facts are virtually irrefutable; it's hard to argue with reality.

The December 2, 1990 issue of the *New York Times* contains an excellent article describing a wager between Julian Simon and Paul Ehrlich. In 1980 (ten years before the article), Simon offered to let anyone pick any natural resource and any future date. Since Simon is of the opinion that resources are actually becoming less scarce due to human ingenuity creating better ways of obtaining them (or cheaper replacements), he was willing to bet anyone that any resources they picked would, factoring in inflation, be *cheaper* in the future than at present.

Ehrlich, upon hearing this proposition, announced that he would "accept Simon's astonishing offer before other greedy people

---

37. Julian L. Simon and Herman Kahn, *The Resourceful Earth* (Oxford, U.K.: Basil Blackwell, 1984).

jump[ed] in." The metals chosen by Ehrlich on the $1,000 wager were chrome, copper, nickel, tin, and tungsten, at the established prices in 1980. The date set for comparison purposes was ten years—hence, 1990. The result: all five metals were significantly cheaper in 1990 than they were in 1980. Without a comment, Ehrlich sent Simon a check to pay off the debt. Simon sent back a thank you along with a new offer to raise the wager to $20,000 pinned to any other resources and any other future date. Ehrlich would not touch this bet, but he nonetheless continued to promote a gloomy view for the world's future. The *New York Times* article was quite positive toward Simon's views. It recounted how Ehrlich's dire predictions of massive deaths by starvation in the world had not come to pass. In fact, it states:

> The number of people affected by famines has been declining steadily during the past three decades. In fact, the number is much lower than it was during the same decades of the last century, even though the world's population is much larger.... Food production has increased faster than population since the publication of *The Population Bomb*, just as it has since the books of Vogt, Osborn, and Malthus.[38]

Encouraging to me is the article's statement that "Among academics, Simon seems to be gaining in the debate. But he is still far behind Ehrlich in winning over the public." Hopefully with this book, and the work of others, even the public will catch up to the truth. It is especially exciting to me (though certainly not surprising) that Simon's conclusions are consistent with the precepts of Scripture. We need not fear overpopulation. God will meet our needs as we obey and don't give up; with God watching over His creation, the universe is *not* a closed system.

---

38. John Tierney, "Betting the Planet," *New York Time*, December 2, 1990, 76.

Part D: The *Decline* of Population in Western Nations

We have seen that more people are not really a detriment to human progress; on the contrary, they actually have the capacity to improve our quality of life. Yet, because of the upside-down, man-centered thinking of the past three decades, millions of people have taken actions to decrease the number of children born—impeding progress, and actually setting the stage for the decline and stagnation of our population and our economy. Not long after Paul Ehrlich was haranguing us with his doomsday tome, *The Population Bomb*, we began to be confronted by an equally disturbing array of books and articles on what has been called the "Birth Dearth."

An article in the *Wall Street Journal* highlights the issue. Entitled "Birth Dearth: Some Thinkers Expect Population to Drop and Trouble to Result,"[39] the article quotes heavily from Ben J. Wattenberg, who has established a reputation for sounding the alarm about the decline of population in Western nations. In his book, also entitled *The Birth Dearth*,[40] Wattenberg, a scholar with the American Enterprise Institute, documents that, "What is happening is this: for about a decade and a half now the peoples in the nations of the free, modern industrial world—that includes us in the U.S.—*have not borne enough children to reproduce themselves over an extended period of time*."[41]

Wattenberg describes the consequences of this fact in two significant areas: (1) our economy and (2) the world geopolitical balance. Regarding the former, he says: "I believe the Birth Dearth will, in the near future, begin to cause turbulence at every level of our economy, from the counters of fast-food restaurants to major corporate board rooms."[42] As to the latter trend, the author predicts:

> I do not mean to sound apocalyptic, but the demographic forces now in motion may just yield a world—one in which we

---

39. "Birth Dearth: Some Thinkers Expect Population to Drop and Trouble to Result," *Wall Street Journal*, June 18, 1987.
40. Ben J. Wattenberg, *The Birth Dearth* (New York: Pharos Books, 1987).
41. Wattenberg, *Birth Dearth*, 6–7.
42. Wattenberg, *Birth Dearth*, 7.

or our own children will live—where the U.S. will no longer be "the most important country in the world." It could be a world where the alliance of Western nations will no longer shape either the political agenda, the culture, or the direction of the global community.[43]

Of course, not all demographers agree with Wattenberg's thesis that we will experience significant problems in our present century due to a lack of children being born. Wattenberg's critics point to the fact that demographers have historically been extremely inaccurate in predicting future fertility trends. Who knows but that couples might start having larger families than before, skewing our best estimates. That certainly is my prayer.

But, humanly speaking, is such a change even probable? The best experts believe that the low fertility rates we have been experiencing in this country since 1973 will continue. Apart from God's intervention, we cannot expect this to change significantly.

Dr. Charles F. Westoff, one of the outstanding fertility experts in the world, predicts that fertility is likely to remain low in our nation due to certain social trends that have been developing in recent years, including:

- the erosion of traditional and religious authority,
- the growth of individualism,
- urbanization,
- the rise of mass education,
- the increasing equality and independence of women, and
- the ideology of consumerism.[44]

He states:

Such social changes, when combined with modern contraceptive technology, in some instances with delayed marriage, and, more recently, with legalized abortion, make very low fertility

---

43. Wattenberg, *Birth Dearth*, 8.
44. Charles F. Westoff, "Fertility Decline in the West: Causes and Prospects," *Population and Development Review*, March 1983, 101.

quite comprehensible.... I do not see any social changes on the horizon that would lead to the expectation that the fertility rate will increase substantially.... More likely is the continuation of rates at or below replacement, and in some instances these rates may indeed fall closer to the one- than to the two-child average. Scattered evidence suggests the proportion of childless women and the proportion with only one child will increase significantly.[45]

Westoff concludes his article with this foreboding comment: "The difficulty is that fertility seems likely to remain precariously low, with the resulting age structure increasing the difficulty of maintaining demographic equilibrium. But one should be cautious with such prognoses—we are moving into largely uncharted territory."[46]

In the late 1980s, an increasing number of newspaper and magazine articles were written about the decline of fertility and the aging of the U.S. population (along with other Western nations). The following quote (from a publication that traditionally has been a propagandist for the "Population Explosion" mentality) underscores the seriousness of the issue of population reversal: "Sometime around 1973, a momentous new demographic phenomenon began to unfold throughout most of the developed world—fertility fell below the level of 2.1 births per woman needed to replace the population in the long run *and remained there*."[47]

We have been so accustomed to being told how fast our world population will double if it grows at x% per year. But just as it will double in about ten years with growth of 7% per year, so will the population decline to half its present number in the space of 10 short years if it *decreases* 7% per year. Population growth is not a foregone conclusion. Some are presently arguing that we are only a few decades away from severe challenges due to under-population.

---

45. Westoff, *Fertility Decline*, 101–102.

46. Westoff, *Fertility Decline*, 103.

47. Leon F. Bouvier, "Planet Earth 1984–2034: A Demographic Vision," *Population Bulletin*, 39, no. 1 (Washington, D.C.: Population Reference Bureau, Inc., 1984), 4.

A more recently published book reviewed in the *Wall Street Journal* on February 7, 2019 is entitled, very simply, *Empty Planet*, written by Canadian social scientist Darrell Bricker along with journalist John Ibbitson. Their premise: "The great defining event of the twenty-first century will occur in three decades, give or take, when the global population starts to decline. Once that decline begins, it will never end."[48] The columnist commenting on the book gives his opinion:

> Their book is a vital warning to the world that the risks associated with population have been catastrophically misread: Governments and activists have spent decades fighting the specter of overpopulation, but now face the looming demographic calamity of global population collapse. Fewer people participating in the economy will mean slower economic growth, less entrepreneurship, rising inequality and calamitous government debt.[49]

All European nations are experiencing a birthrate lower than the 2.1 children per woman needed to replace the nation's population in the long run. Of course, this may change soon. With the immigration of Muslims along with their relatively large families, the character of Europe is in the process of major change.

In response to Europe's native population decline, a number of European nations have taken economic steps to try to encourage the birth of more children. Already in the mid-1980s, the German Parliament passed legislation aimed at giving a tax break and subsidizing women who would set aside their careers in order to bear children. The result has been disheartening for German officials. Birth rates have continued to spiral down even after the implementation of the economic package. One German explained

---

48. Lyman Stone, "A Drop in Numbers," *Wall Street Journal*, February 7, 2019.
49. Stone, "A Drop in Numbers," *Wall Street Journal*.

his reaction: "The aid is too minuscule. Anyway, you can't pay Germans to have kids."[50]

The French have a similar economic plan to pay families for each child, beginning in the third month of pregnancy, through the ninth month after birth. It also seems to be ineffective. Comparable programs have been equally ineffective in Eastern European nations like Bulgaria and Hungary, who also face declining populations.[51]

Similar problems are being felt in Japan. The Detroit *Free Press* described the specter of economic and social difficulties as a result of the plunging Japanese birth rate. The current fertility rate there is 1.57 births per woman, far below the 2.1 break-even point. "Bureaucrats and business leaders are aware of the problem, since Japan's economic system rests on a combination of technological prowess and the energies of a young work force."[52] If current trends continue, Japan's current population of 127 million will drop below 100 million by 2049 with one in three citizens there considered elderly.[53]

How about the United States? Except for a mini-upturn in 1990, we have been seeing a reduction in our fertility rate since 1973 (the year abortion was legalized). In 2017 alone, American women had the lowest birth rate ever recorded. Deaths now outnumber births among white people in more than half of the states in our nation due to insufficient numbers of babies being born.[54] Due to this reality and other factors, the U. S. Census Bureau predicts our population will soon begin to decline for the first time in our history. With the scenario it considers most likely to occur, the Census Bureau predicts the U. S. population will slowly grow to 302 million people in 2038 and then begin to experience "negative growth" (translated

50. "Worried West Germany Tries to Get Parents Producing Children Again," *Grand Rapids Press*, October 2, 1985.

51. Bouvier, *Planet Earth*, 20.

52. "Fewer births haunt Japan," *Detroit Free Press,* July 31, 1991.

53. Sasha Ingber, "Japan's Population Is in Rapid Decline," *National Public Radio*, December 21, 2018.

54. Sabrina Tavernise, "Fewer Births Than Deaths Among Whites in Majority of U.S. States," *New York Times*, June 21, 2018, A1.

"decline"). This decline will occur despite significant immigration accounting for more than one half of the additions to our population in the year 2020. Even factoring in these immigrants, deaths will still begin to outnumber both immigration and births by the year 2038.[55]

Related to the issue of deaths outnumbering births and immigration is another demographic fact: the elderly are the fastest growing segment of our nation. Alan Pifer, head of the Carnegie Corporation's Aging Society Project, was quoted as expressing significant concerns about the "graying of America": "Specifically, two 'separate and simultaneous events' account for a rapidly aging America: 'the speed with which the number of older and very old people is growing, and the dramatic decline in the proportion of young people, a decline expected to continue in the decades ahead.'"[56]

As another indicator of this trend, as of late 1984, those over 65 in the U.S. outnumbered teenagers for the first time in the entire history of the U.S. By 2025, those over 65 will outnumber teens by a 2 to 1 margin! The relative numbers of "old" people (over 85) was insignificant in 1900, but is expected to surpass 15 million by 2050, having grown to over 5% of our population.[57] The result? Since we already have the beginnings of euthanasia occurring in our nation, imagine how the pressure for this practice will grow as we increasingly feel the weight of an enormous elderly population with their manifold health needs. In the words of Ronald J. Vogel, economist and public policy specialist at the University of Arizona in Tucson:

---

55. "People Patterns," *Wall Street Journal*, February 7, 1989, using data compiled from *American Demographics* magazine. Also see: U. S. Bureau of the Census, Current Population Reports, series P-25, no. 1018, *Projections of the Population of the U. S. by Age, Sex and Race: 1988 to 2080* (Washington, D.C., U. S. Government Printing Office, 1989).

56. "Eying an Elderly Outlook," *Grand Rapids Press*, June 19, 1986.

57. "The Oldest Old," *Wall Street Journal*, July 30, 1984.

There are likely to be fewer medical services, more chronic ill-ness, and even economic "warfare" between the generations—serious enough to possibly destabilize the country.... That's what happens in a country where too many people depend on too few people and where large numbers of non-productive old people must be financially and medically supported by taxing the young workers.[58]

News reports recently announced that Medicare and Social Security are swiftly moving towards insolvency due to the shrinking working population.[59] As the number of elderly swells and the num-ber of children declines, the likelihood that our national concern for children in general will ebb becomes a greater certainty. In 1960, children under 18 represented 36% of our population, and hence demanded much attention by our society. By 2050, the percent-age of children is expected to drop to 20% of our population while the elderly over 65 will grow from its present 11% to over 21% of the population.

In some ways, children and the elderly always compete for scarce resources. But who will win in the future? Obviously the "gray power, condo commandos" with the dollars, votes, time, and political connections, will have much more impact than the rela-tively legally disenfranchised children will. And who really cares about the future when so few of the citizens alive will ever live to experience it? In reality, the average middle-aged wage earner will probably have disdain for both groups and do all in his power to reduce the number of children needing services as well as the num-ber of elderly.

In addition to the uncharitable competition that will likely grow between the generations, changing demographics will also affect the relative influence of various ethnic groups in our cul-ture. As a result of immigration and lowering birthrates for white

---

58. "Grim Future Seen for 'Baby Boomers' Born in 1945–1965," *Grand Rapids Press*, October 3, 1983.

59. Gabrielle Levy, "Analysts: Medicare Insolvency Looms, But Social Secu-rity Poses Bigger Threat," *U.S. News and World Report*, June 13, 2018.

Americans, it is projected that non-white Americans under the age of 18 will outnumber white Americans under 18 by the early 2020s. And white Americans of all ages will become a minority starting in 2045.[60] On the other end of the spectrum are Jewish Americans. At the turn of the century, Jews and Roman Catholics generally earned the reputation of having large families. A number of Orthodox Jewish families continue the tradition of having large numbers of children in what they consider to be obedience to God. But the vast majority of American Jews today are less in tune with scriptural principles and place a low priority on childbearing. The results are astounding: while there are currently about 5.3 million Jewish Americans in the U.S., it is projected (by Elihu Bergman, formerly of the Harvard Center for Population Studies) that, if present trends continue, this number will decline to only about 420,000 by the year 2076. This decline to less than a tenth of their present numbers is due to the simple fact that Jewish couples marry later, are more likely to remain single than the population as a whole, and that Jewish women are more likely to defer childbearing and limit family size due to career aspirations.[61] Some experts estimate the average Jewish woman has only 1.3 to 1.5 children, far fewer than the 2.1 necessary to "break even."

"So what," someone may say, "who needs American Jews anyhow?" While Jewish people comprise only about 1.4% of our current population (and 0.2% of our population in 60 years if present trends continue), they represent an inordinately high percentage of our nation's scientists, artists, performers, and entrepreneurs. For example, 20% of our Nobel laureates have been Jewish. Our nation would lose much from the absence of these talented people.

On the other extreme (numbers-wise) are the Mormons, who continue to grow faster than almost any other segment of our nation. Utah, the bastion of Mormonism, has grown 45% since 1970, due

---

60. William H. Frey, "The US will become 'minority white' in 2045, Census projects," *The Avenue* from the Brookings Institute, updated September 10, 2018.

61. "American Judaism: As Jewish Population Falls in U.S., Leaders Seek to Reverse Trend," *Wall Street Journal*, April 13, 1984.

to women in that state bearing children at twice the national average.[62] One result of this ongoing "baby boom" in Utah is that as of 2016, Utah has the lowest median age in the country (29.2 years) compared to the national median of more than 38. But perhaps the most significant result of this population growth will undoubtedly be a greater Mormon impact on the culture of our country.

Anyone who travels to Utah cannot help but see that the Mormon faith and belief system has a large impact on the government, media, and other aspects of that state's life. My wife and I were in the Salt Lake City area for a television interview a number of years ago. We had some extra time and spent it browsing at a suburban shopping mall (my wife's idea, I assure you!). We were amazed at the number of babies in strollers as well as the large number of pregnant women everywhere.

The apparent morality of many Mormons is highly commendable, but as a believer in the Bible, I do not desire that their theology be widely disseminated, since I believe that it often departs seriously from the truth of God's Word. Yet the Mormons' numerical growth, which exceeds most other religions, almost guarantees their growing influence in the years to come. In no way am I trying to discourage Mormons from having large families. Our nation needs people regardless of their religious perspectives, if for no other reason than to keep our economy moving into the future. But I am wondering if evangelical Christians will do their part to respond to this challenge.

As Mary Pride points out, Christians, by having larger families, could soon have a very significant influence on our culture— provided, of course, that we raise our children in godly ways. But if we continue to follow the example provided by our increasingly secularized culture in which we value career and other priorities more than having additional children, our influence will most likely decline, along with our numbers.

---

62. "As the Nation Ages, Utah Gets Younger, Thanks to Mormons," *Wall Street Journal*, November 11, 1984.

Besides changes in the ethnic make-up of our country, and the serious concerns raised by a growing percentage of elderly people, our economy itself is already suffering from a lack of sufficient population growth and is likely only to get worse in the future. Experts point to a growing shortage of unskilled labor in our country that typically is filled by young people accepting entry-level jobs. This is good news for our children looking for part-time employment (as the wages are driven up), but it is also bad news for business and our economy as a whole if we wish to remain competitive in the world market. Employers are having to turn to other, less desirable employees: "As the supply of young workers dwindles, U.S. employers could be forced to recruit the sort of applicants they have shunned in the past: social misfits, the illiterate and untrained."[63]

As another approach, some corporations have been investing large sums of money to help train under-educated potential employees. Unless these efforts work, as our population stops growing, and begins to decline in numbers, the ability of many businesses to expand (and some to even survive) will be questionable. Our economic growth is at least in part predicated on the expectancy of growing markets. On a global basis, we seem to have a glut of industrial over-capacity in the production of autos, steel, computers, and many other items.[64] Hence, there is the growing apprehension of a worldwide recession fueled at least in part by stagnating populations in virtually all Western nations.

Consider the economic impact if the average woman had 2.8 children instead of the approximately 1.8 that we have seen during the past four decades. In rough numbers, assuming the current approximately four million babies born per year, we would have more like 6.2 million children born per year, resulting in 88 million more young people in our nation. Think of the economic impact of such a baby boom! While not all would be positive in the short

---

63. "Report Cites Need to Hire Misfits of Workforce," *Grand Rapids Press*, July 28, 1985.

64. "Glutted Markets: A Global Overcapacity Hurts Many Industries; No Easy Cure Seen," *Wall Street Journal*, March 9, 1987.

run, we are talking about a lot of people able to use their skills in the labor market and to consume items our businesses are trying hard to sell. We are simply talking at this juncture about pragmatic issues that involve dollars and cents, but God uses common things like money to get missionaries sent around the world. Furthermore, what about the profound spiritual value of 88 million unique children created in the image of God? It's beyond comprehension!

Allen C. Carlson, a widely quoted author and lecturer for the pro-family Rockford Institute, argues persuasively that children are a real boon to a free nation's economy.[65] Carlson rightly criticizes Malthusian thinking as a sort of "intellectual herpes" that chronically reappears in various parts of the body politic, causing great consternation and confusion. Dr. Carlson has shown how the 1.5 million per year aborted American children, if allowed to live, could effectively cancel out the ravages of our current national debt. While the numbers he comes up with may initially appear astounding, Carlson's logic is reasonable. In his calculations, Carlson assumes that children are a net economic drain until age 18, when many will then begin to be "average" producers of goods and services (as well as providing a market for the production of goods and services). Upon reaching 18, the 1.5 million "non-aborted" children in Carlson's model would provide a net annual increase in our national income of over $49 billion![66] Conservatively, a fairly substantial portion of this income would end up in government coffers, thereby helping to reduce our exorbitant national debt. But if we add to the impact of these "non-aborted" children and also include those children "planned" out of existence by their upscale parents with their pills, diaphragms, condoms, vasectomies, and tubal ligations, we will quickly come up with even more astounding economic numbers.

---

65. Allen C. Carlson, "The Malthusian Budget Deficit," *The Human Life Review*, Summer 1985, 35.

66. Carlson, *Budget Deficit*, 45.

Let me put it this way: Would you rather live in a city or state that is growing in population, or one that is declining? Would you choose a locale where the average age of its citizens is growing older, or one in which there are lots of young, energetic people? Most of us are drawn toward growth, people, and energy. It is hard to imagine what good times we could be having as a nation if we were still growing with God. Older Americans remember the post-WWII baby boom time of real economic growth, general stability, and blessing in our nation. Those days are now long gone. We are in a decline. Unless there is a change, it will be just a matter of time before economic chaos unravels the decaying fabric of this great nation. While children cannot produce a healthy economy by themselves, they are at least one critical element necessary for a growing economy.

Part E: Final Thoughts on Population

Despite the significant and seemingly irreversible population decline in developed Western nations, many people feel the less developed "third world" countries will more than make up the difference. They are therefore still concerned about world-wide overpopulation.

It is true that population in many developing countries continues to increase. But in 1984, the growth rate in the world as a whole declined from 2% per year to 1.7% per year, the first decline in modern history.[67] Since 1984, the world population growth rate has continued to fall every year, reaching an all-time low of 1.07% in 2019.[68] This reflects not only the population downturn in developed nations, but also a slowing down of the increase in third world countries as well.

But isn't there massive starvation due to overpopulation? No. During the period from 1961 through 1980, developing countries, lumped together, showed an annual increase in food production

---

67. "Population Growth Rate Drops for First Time in Modern History," *Grand Rapids Press*, June 13, 1984.

68. https://www.worldometers.info/world-population/#growthrate

of 3.1 percent, "comfortably above the average annual population growth rate of 2.4 percent."[69] That pattern continues to the present. According to multiple studies, the world's farmers today produce enough food to feed 1.5 times the current world's population.[70]

Yet we have all seen the ravages of famines in third world countries. Isn't "overpopulation" the culprit? No! If you look more closely at the famines that have devastated these parts of the world, you can see that governmental mismanagement or corruption (or both) have been significant factors. Even trendy *Newsweek* offered the following comment on Africa's 1984 famine:

> Who's to blame for Africa's crisis? Nature certainly accounts for a good deal of it. But the drought, as devastating as it has been, is only part of the story. The destruction and dislocation it has brought could have been mitigated if African leaders had served their nations well before the drought.... As it is, many of the leaders mismanaged economies, squandered national wealth, and literally threw away the future as they jostled with one another for personal power and gain.... It has taken African leaders quite a long time to come around to accepting the fact that many of the continent's pains are self-inflicted.[71]

Similar blame should rightly fall on the leadership of South America's formerly most prosperous nation, Venezuela, a nation that now struggles to feed its people due to governmental incompetence and greed. Blaming population for famine is like blaming the innocent people of a large city for its high murder rate. Obviously, if there were no people in the city, there would be less crime. But let's blame the real culprits—the offenders, not the potential victims.

---

69. Peter Hendry, "Food and Population: Beyond Five Billion," *Population Bulletin*, 43, no. 2 (Washington, D. C.: Population Reference Bureau, Inc., April, 1988).

70. https://medium.com/@jeremyerdman/we-produce-enough-food-to-feed -10-billion-people-so-why-does-hunger-still-exist-8086d2657539

71. Hilary Ng'weno, "Placing the Blame," *Newsweek*, November 26, 1984, 55.

Finally, there are diseases that threaten what population growth (both here and abroad) we might otherwise experience. Acquired Immunity Disease Syndrome (AIDS) claimed the lives of over 675,000 people in the United States since the beginning of this epidemic.[72] The prospects in Africa are even worse. There, where it is felt the disease originated, AIDS is being passed into the general population also by heterosexual contacts. As recently as 2012, there were 23.8 million Africans infected with the AIDS virus, with over one million adults and children dying from the disease annually.[73]

And what other diseases like AIDS are lurking beneath the surface? We too often assume that medical science will somehow protect us from all harm and ensure our indefinite continuation. But there are any number of human and "natural" threats to our very existence that could easily send the world population plummeting downward. Certainly one should not choose to avoid having children because of the fear that it will directly or indirectly impact starving people in South America or Africa.

How about the issue of climate change and environmental issues that is being made so much of today by the Green Lobby? The same advocates of doom and gloom regarding the feared population explosion tend also to be the forefront of the "Green Party" movement in recent years. Their goal, very simply, is to cooperate with the media to discredit scientists with differing viewpoints, and to convince the public to put its faith in their erudite pronouncements. When you possess the power to protect the "environment," you have the power to virtually control everything, whether on private or public property.[74]

Julian Simon expressed it well when he said that we must certainly work on keeping our planet as tidy as possible, but the facts speak quite powerfully that we haven't let everything go completely

---

72. https://en.wikipedia.org/wiki/HIV/AIDS_in_the_United_States

73. https://www.dosomething.org/us/facts/11-facts-about-hiv-africa

74. For an excellent article on this subject, see Edward C. Krug, "Save the Planet, Sacrifice the People: The Environmental Party's Bid for Power," *Imprimis* (Hillsdale College), July 1991.

to the dogs. The average life expectancy of humans continues to climb, giving at least indirect support to the premise that our planet is healthier to live in now than it was in the days of our ancestors. Groups can always inundate us with scare stories, but we should not be excessively lured by the "return to nature" pitch which for many of the "Green" groups seems to elevate trees, animals, and even rocks above mankind. What is more important, a house, or the people who live in the house? Obviously, the people are more important. As a person who owns a house, I like to keep it fairly neat, clean, and orderly, but not to the detriment of the much more important people who live in it. In a similar way, we want to keep our world relatively neat, clean, and orderly, but not to the detriment of the much more important people who reside in it.

And let's not forget that our sovereign God has already decreed in Isaiah 51:6, "The earth will grow old like a garment, and those who dwell in it will die in like manner." We learn elsewhere in Isaiah that God is creating a new heaven and a new earth. Though sin has irreversibly tainted this universe, God will graciously make a new one someday. While we should not unnecessarily cause ecological damage to our planet by the way we live but should exercise good stewardship since we respect it deeply as God's creation, we also should not be afraid to "subdue" the earth and have dominion over it, knowing that the God who commanded this is the same one who, in the proper time, will certainly create a new heaven and a new earth.

What can we conclude from this lengthy discussion of the overpopulation issue? Can anyone irrefutably say that we have an overpopulated world to the extent that we should forego having children as a consequence? By no means! In fact, the very opposite is true. We have a dearth of children in this country and in the world as a whole. Do we really have too many people for this life, not to mention for God's eternal kingdom in heaven? The standing orders of God to be fruitful and multiply still apply, despite the teachings of some short-sighted thinkers to the contrary. We have a long way to go before we comply with God's instructions to fill the earth.

Part Four

CONCLUSION

CHAPTER 19

Changing Our World
One Family at a Time

Until about fifty years ago, we had beautiful diversity in the size of families in America. It was common to know of families with no children, others with one or two children, and still others having upwards of eight, ten, or even twelve children. The average family had about four. By comparison, today, families with more than four children are increasingly rare; most families have between one and three offspring, with the national average currently at two.

Homes with big families who follow God are among the most exciting places on earth—in my opinion, far more exciting than Disneyland. Just imagine living close to ten different personalities, each possessing all the creative potential and ideas of a person created in God's image. Imagine being loved and appreciated (at least *some* of the time) by a large variety of special people whom you will know in this life until death separates you from them. What an incredible benefit for each person in the family!

Everywhere I go to speak on this issue, there are always a number of people who will wait to speak to me afterwards because they want to tell me about their wonderful experience of growing up in a large family. They usually add how fun it continues to be to get together at special times with their siblings. I remember one young man recounting the large families that both of his parents came from. He told how virtually all the members of both of these families had chosen to continue living near each other as they "settled down." Every Sunday after church, their respective families continued to gather at a brother or sister's home for wonderful fellowship. This young man bemoaned the fact that he now lived too far away from the others to be able to attend these weekly gatherings. "They are the *most* enjoyable times," he said wistfully. I have three wonderful sisters, and I enjoy seeing them two or three times per year. But our dozen children love connecting daily with each other in texts, emails, and phone calls, with a passion that amazes me. And when we get the entire family together, the joy they express is way over the top!

Because we were made by God for having relationships with others, *people*—not things, not careers, not money—should be the most important thing (under God) to us in this life. I figure there are more than one hundred different one-on-one relationships in our family of twelve children and two adults. It is *so* helpful for our children to learn how to get along with all the others. I didn't say it was always easy—it isn't. But it is helpful and enriching for each one.

Being one of a dozen children also helps each child realize that, while he or she has unique skills, abilities, and personality traits, he or she is not the center of the universe. They must all learn to balance their own desires for the sake of others. I'm learning that there is a "big family system" which develops in healthy large families as the family members adjust to the demands both inside and outside the family. It's exciting to hear the experiences of other large families as they struggle with issues common to all large families.

In the Jewish community, it is the Orthodox group (those holding to scriptural absolutes) who often have large families. In a very upbeat article found in the *Hadassah Magazine*, three large Israeli families are highlighted.[1] I love the comments by Dina Weinberg who is described as an "attractive, elegant, incredibly slim" mother of twelve children. She says,

> So many people are looking for transcendental thrills. They search the world for pleasure that lasts. But for me real pleasure

---

1. Helen Davis and Carol Grootter, "Easier by the Dozen," *Hadassah Magazine*, December, 1982.

is to have, hold, rear children. They are so pure. To be in contact with a child is a spiritual experience.... You know, the
greatest *mitzvah* is to save life. Of how much more importance
is it, then, to create a life?.... [Other people] expect 12 children
to be deprived in some way—physically, emotionally, or mentally. Instead, they see fine children, lacking nothing as far as
personality and emotional development is concerned, who are
growing up in an atmosphere of tremendous love, caring, and
mutual respect.... It's my role to be a housewife—to build a
home.... In a regular job—whether in an office or someplace
else—anyone can do someone else's work. But no one else can
have my child except me. I was given the strength and health
to have children. Everyone has to do what he or she can do.

The authors of the article asked Mrs. Weinberg what she says
to people who are struggling with only two or three children. She
laughs and points out that she, too, was once the mother of two and
three children and knows how it feels. But, "this too shall pass":

I think I am a better parent today than I was when my eldest
children were small. I feel quite guilty about it, in fact. The
love, the patience, the understanding grows with each child.
You become aware of the overall span of childhood, of cause
and effect, and this enables you to react to later children with
much greater sensitivity.... I find I am automatically aware
of each child's moods. Even in the morning chaos of getting
everyone dressed and fed and off to school, I'm registering that
that one is dawdling, and this one is a little pale, and another
is in a great rush—and wondering why.... Remember, I don't
have 12 *little* children. The older children help the younger
ones and they all begin helping in the house as soon as they
are able to do so. They have to help themselves, each other,
and me, or it wouldn't work. Besides this is healthy training
for them. A child who grows up knowing how to give and take
will be a better wife, husband, parent and citizen later.

The article also contains similar comments from two other mothers, one having nineteen children and the other ten. I particularly

liked the view of Mrs. Hannah Siegel who looked backwards to the time when she had only two children:

> When the second [child] was born, I thought I'd never manage. And it was really only after the fourth that things got easier. I don't know why. Maybe I just grew into the job, became more organized, [and] learned to do with less sleep.

As a former juvenile court judge, I often saw wonderful families who have adopted large numbers of multi-handicapped and racially mixed children. One such outstanding Christian family, Bob and Janet Schout, and their twelve adopted children, comes to mind. What joy there was in my courtroom when we confirmed their tenth adoption. Janet—herself one of twelve children but, in God's providence, physically unable to bear children biologically—told me: "God meant for some children to be removed from their biological parents so that they can be entrusted into the care of adoptive parents, and thereby, achieve purpose in their lives."

In 1990, Marcia and I had the privilege of sharing what God had been teaching us about the joys of a large family with Dr. James Dobson and his Focus on the Family radio audience. The two programs we recorded aired that year and were re-broadcast in 1994. Dobson reported that many couples subsequently wrote him to say they had changed their perspectives on having additional children as a result of the programs, for which we give all the glory to God.

Many years later, just before Christmas in 2015, we received a large package in the mail from the Bontrager family who live in Iowa. While we have yet to personally meet them, each member of the family—consisting of dad and mom and ten children—wrote us a handwritten note of thanks. Apparently, many years before, the mother of this family, Becky Bontrager, heard our program on Focus and became convicted about her perspectives on having Christ be Lord of her family size. Up to that point, she and her husband, Marlin, were planning on having at most three children. In her own words:

Because of the radio interview that you had with Dr. James Dobson over 20 years ago, my husband and I gave up our plans to choose how many children we would have. There were many times that I, as a mother of 10 children born in 16 years, was overwhelmed and totally exhausted and even afraid; but I can testify that every time I called on the Lord, He was my strength and song.... Truly He has blessed our family exceeding abundantly above all things.... With deep gratitude for the difference your message had in my life. I want to encourage you to continue to proclaim God's ways and His goodness.

The husband, Marlin Bontrager, confessed this in his letter to me:

I realized I had been much more anti-abortion than pro-life. We always wanted a family, but never thought about the blessing of having God provide and direct. As a father, I realize how your message totally changed our life, and through your ministry many others as well.

Marlin is referring to the fact that his family now travels the country as "The Bontrager Family Singers."

As I recently re-read the letters written by the Bontrager children, I was driven to tears. It struck me, what a joy these precious children must bring to our heavenly Father! And what an impact they are already having on our world! Listen to the words of dear Rebecca Bontrager, the "baby" of the family:

Thank you for speaking on the blessing of children. I am the youngest in our family of 10 children, and without your message, I might not be here. Our family has been able to encourage other families to have more children. Keep encouraging families!

Finally, listen to seventh-born Taylor's perspectives:

Many parents see children as a temporary bother instead of those that God can use to serve Him. If everyone who could would receive as many children as God would give them and raise them to love God and His Word, the effect would be thousands of young people passionate about serving God.

Final Words

Children are messages we send to a time and a place we ourselves cannot go. Children are work, expensive, even painful at times. But they are people created in the image of God with the ability to greatly influence life on this planet and, by the converting grace of our covenant God, the potential of living forever in His eternal kingdom. So why do we think the idea of bearing and raising another child is all about us? And why do we preach about Jesus being Lord of every area of life except this area of family size? Friends, this is huge. Yes, it's not easy. It's scary. I've been there. But I could weep for the rest of my life knowing what I now know about the incredible children God chose to create through Marcia and me, if we had instead decided to say no.

The challenge is there for you. Will you allow Jesus to be Lord of your family size for His glory, for the blessing of our nation and His kingdom, and for your ultimate joy?

APPENDIXES

On Birth Control

Herein is my Father glorified, that ye bear
much fruit; and so shall ye be my disciples.
                                            —John 15:8

Ah, yes! This question of birth control agitates the minds of many Christian friends. Some say that we, Christian women, have duties to perform other than bearing and rearing children; that we must also tend to mission work for the sake of extending the Lord's kingdom to every part of the world. For we must bear much fruit to the glory of our heavenly Father and the Lord Jesus Christ. He, our Savior, said so when He departed for glory: "Go ye forth into all the world...!"

Yes, indeed! But did He not add, "beginning from Jerusalem"? And has He not promised to own my children? If He then will give me many children, if I bear much fruit, being in Him, will not the Father be glorified therein? May not I, myself, then contribute directly to the coming of His kingdom? Having this promise that He will adopt my children for His very own, is not my first duty to bear for Him as many as it may please Him to give unto me?

Some say it is not necessary that I have many children.... I must guard my health, conserve my strength, look out for myself, and for my family. [But] when I am conscious of abiding in Him, and experience His blessed presence in me, then I dare not think of preventing the birth of a child He may want me to receive from Him and to bring up for Him.

And must I care for my own life? Does not the Master say that "whosoever seeketh to save his life shall lose it?" Or again, shall I try to safeguard my own life in order that I may have energy and leisure to help send forth more missionaries into heathen lands where they may jeopardize their precious lives in the service of the Master? But, still! How do I know that my Lord may not, perhaps, deign to select the child whose birth I would prevent as one of His missionaries to carry the message to foreign lands? And, oh! That would be interest thrice doubly compounded upon my little capital of loving devotion—upon my talents which He gave me to put them to usury!

Ah, some say there are heavy burdens to bear in the rearing of children as well as grave risks in bringing them into the world! Yes, yes, indeed; but my Master says: "If ye abide in me, and my words abide in you, ask whatsoever ye will, and it shall be done unto you."—Ah, then, Lord, give me children, many, to bring up for thee that I may be always abounding in the work of the Lord, my and my children's Redeemer!

Should I shirk my own duty denying my service to my Lord, that I might labor to send others? Should I protect my own life and health in order to give others the opportunity to risk theirs for the Master?

Moreover, has not the Father himself provided a distribution of gifts and of labor such that, while I and others with me are almost exclusively occupied with the duties and burdens of motherhood, these other tasks need not and will not be neglected? Are there not many of my sisters in the Lord from whom He, in His divine wisdom, has kept the blessed joys and the sweet burdens of motherhood?

Who then dares presume to interfere with the Father's dispensation of gifts and of tasks? Who dares to limit, arbitrarily, the operation of His wonderful powers?

"Theophila"

Taken from *The Banner*, July 24, 1936

"His Number"
by Janet Carlton

While waiting as a bride to be
I heard God firmly speak to me,
To cast aside the world's device
And become a living sacrifice.
Namely that my womb should bear
The ones He planned to cradle there,
Lest some humanistic creed
Eliminate His godly seed.

How I wrestled with that word—
So unusual. So absurd!
Would God...could God take control
And what would His requirements hold?

After much debate and doubt,
I threw my own decisions out.
If God can measure earth and sea,
Can He not chart a family?
And if He names and numbers stars
Then in His book is each of ours.
Therefore, we gave to Him the right
To build the house and take the charge.

A mother now with six on hand,
By faith and grace I have no plan,
But cast aside the things that kill
To let His number be fulfilled.

Children

by Henry Wadsworth Longfellow

Come to me, O ye children!
   For I hear you at your play,
And the questions that perplexed me
   Have vanished quite away.

Ye open the eastern windows,
   That look towards the sun,
Where thoughts are singing swallows,
   And the brooks of morning run.

In your hearts are the birds and the sunshine,
   In your thoughts the brooklet's flow,
But in mine is the wind of autumn,
   And the first fall of the snow.

Ah, what would the world be to us
   If the children were no more?
We should dread the desert behind us
   Worse than the dark before.

What the leaves are to the forest,
   With light and air for food,
Ere their sweet and tender juices
   Have been hardened into wood,

That to the world are children;
   Through them it feels the glow
Of a brighter and sunnier climate
   Than reaches the trunks below.

Come to me, O ye children!
   And whisper in my ear
What the birds and the winds are singing
   In your sunny atmosphere.

For what are all our contrivings
   And the wisdom of our books,
When compared with your caresses,
   And the gladness of your looks?

Ye are better than all the ballads
   That ever were sung or said;
For ye are living poems,
   And all the rest are dead.

From: *Best Loved Poems* by Henry Wadsworth Longfellow,
Peoples Book Club, Chicago, 1949.